RETURNING A
BORROWED
TONGUE

POEMS BY FILIPINO AND FILIPINO AMERICAN WRITERS

RETURNING A BORROWED TONGUE

EDITED AND WITH AN INTRODUCTION BY NICK CARBÓ

:: COFFEE HOUSE PRESS :: MINNEAPOLIS

Acknowledgements to the publishers and authors for the work published in this book appear on page 235, following the text, and shall constitute a continuation of the acknowledgements page.

Cover photo: "Ifugao Barbie, #1" © 1995 by cyn. zarco. Used with permission from the photographer.

Cover and book design by Jinger Peissig.

This project has been made possible through a major grant from the Star Tribune/Cowles Media Company. Additional support has been provided by the Minnesota State Arts Board, through an appropriation by the Minnesota State Legislature; the National Endowment for the Arts; the Lila Wallace-Reader's Digest Fund; The McKnight Foundation; Lannan Foundation; Jerome Foundation; Target Stores, Dayton's, and Mervyn's by the Dayton Hudson Foundation; General Mills Foundation; St. Paul Companies; Honeywell Foundation; Beverly J. and John A. Rollwagen Fund of The Minneapolis Foundation; Prudential Foundation; and The Andrew W. Mellon Foundation.

Coffee House Press books are available to the trade through our primary distributor, Consortium Book Sales & Distribution, 1045 Westgate Drive, Saint Paul, MN 55114. For personal orders, catalogs or other information, write to: Coffee House Press, 27 North Fourth Street, Suite 400, Minneapolis, MN 55401

Library of Congress CIP Data
Retruning a borrowed tongue /
edited and with an introduction by Nick Carbó.
     p.   cm.
  At head of title: Poems by Filipino and Filipino-Amercan writers.
  Includes bibliographical references.
   ISBN 1-56689-043-8 (pbk.)
   1. Philippine poetry (English) 2. American poetry—
Filipino American authors. 3. Filipino Amercans—Poetry.
   4. Philippines—Poetry. I. Carbó, Nick, 1964-.
PR9550.6.R48   1995
821—DC20   96-11376
                                          CIP

10   9   8   7   6   5   4   3   2   1

CONTENTS

In memory of
Bienvenido N. Santos
(1911-1996)

Returning a Borrowed Tongue

AN INTRODUCTION BY NICK CARBÓ

The more than 7,000 islands that comprise the Philippine Archipelago extend like a string of emeralds on the northeastern edge of South East Asia. They are bounded on the north and east by the Pacific Ocean, on the south by the Celebes Sea, and on the west by the South China Sea. Dr. Jose Rizal, the Filipino national hero martyred during the revolution against Spain, romantically referred to this archipelago as *la perla del mar de oriente* or pearl of the orient sea. The archipelago is part of the western Pacific Rim of Fire and more than twelve active volcanos periodically erupt in bombastic displays of fiery lava and plumes of ash. There are devastating earthquakes, floods of biblical proportions, and typhoons that wipe out whole villages. These sensational images of natural disasters make good copy for newspaper reports and most of what Americans have learned about the Philippines is connected to one sort of disaster or another. Not much is known about the country's complex history, its diverse cultures, and its literature.

The earliest known human fossils found in the Philippines were discovered in the Tabon Caves on the westernmost island of Palawan. These fossils are about 22,000 years old, suggesting that the first human migrations into the islands occurred during the Late Pleistocene of the last Ice Age. Physical anthropologists have determined that these human fossils share the characteristics of modern man, *homo erectus*. The succeeding waves of migration to the archipelago were those of people of Mongoloid stock. By the third century B.C., these inhabitants were goldsmithing, making pottery, weaving cloth, building sailing vessels, and trading with ports as far away as China, Champa (Vietnam), and Malacca.

The written history of the archipelago began in 1521 with the arrival of Ferdinand Magellan, who was sailing under the Spanish Crown. Magellan was eventually killed in a skirmish with the warriors of Lapu Lapu, the leader of the island of Mactan. In 1543 Ruy Gómez de Villalobos set sail from Mexico to establish a colony in the archipelago. The expedition ended up in utter failure except that Villalobos was able to give the islands a name, *Las Islas Filipinas,* after the crown prince *Felipe Segundo,* or Phillip the Second. In 1565 Miguel Lopez de Legazpi established a permanent Spanish presence on the island of Cebu. In 1571 he sailed north towards Luzon and captured the city of Manila from a local Muslim potentate. Manila was then made the capital of the archipelago. From this point on the Spanish Empire colonized and controlled the islands for more than three hundred years.

The entrance of the United States into Philippine affairs began with the Spanish-American War in 1898. The Spanish possessions of Cuba, Puerto Rico, and the Philippines were lost to the u.s. With the signing of the Treaty of Paris later that year, the Spanish government agreed to cede the Philippine Archipelago to the United States. This agreement cost the u.s. $20,000,000. The native population of the Philippines did not accept this change in colonial masters with open arms. By the end of the nineteenth century, the Filipinos were well on their way towards a Filipino national identity with hopes of achieving independence from Spain. In 1896 a secret society called the Katipunan led the revolt against Spain. The independence of the first Philippine Republic was proclaimed in 1898 and the first republican government in Asia was formed. But having just paid twenty million dollars for this new territory, the u.s. could not morally and financially afford to lose its investment in prime Pacific real estate. The government of President McKinley decided to ignore the sovereign rights of this newly declared independent republic. Realizing the United State's true intent of taking the archipelago for themselves, the Filipinos resisted this new enemy in the Philippine-American War from 1899 to 1902. During this conflict, the Filipino population suffered more then a million losses under the might of an emerging industrial and military giant. The United States not only won on the military battlefield, but also on the cultural and linguistic terrain in their attempt at colonizing their newly found colonial subjects.

When one considers the historical factors of America's colonization, that its language, its cultural and its educational institutions were imposed (in the guise of the policy of Benevolent Assimilation) on a native Filipino population, a pattern of dominance/subjugation and superiority/inferiority begins to emerge. Emilio Aguinaldo, the President of the first Philippine Republic and main "Insurrecto" leader, was captured in 1901 by Frederick Funston. Within that same year, the u.s. transport ship *Thomas* arrived in Manila Bay carrying five hundred young American teachers whose mission was to "educate, uplift, and civilize" the Filipinos. The English spoken by Americans spread across the Philippines and quickly took root as the preferred language for education, administration, commerce, and daily living. So, by 1910, u.s. officials claimed that more Filipinos could read, write, and speak English than any other single language. For the next forty years, American culture and its language assumed a dominant position in the life of Filipinos. The transmission of culture was undoubtedly one-sided. Many indigenous expressions remained hidden and were suppressed because of their presumed inferiority.

The period between 1900 to 1940 is generally considered a period of tutelage under the Americans. Filipinos were seen as mere students of English, and thus their early literary efforts in the language were not always taken seriously. It is important to note, however, that the American teaching efforts did not include creative writing. As the Filipino critic Gemino Abad points out: ". . . it is a little misleading to speak of a literary apprenticeship during those first forty years because we already had accomplished writers in Spanish, Tagalog, and other native languages. The apprenticeship was linguistic and cultural, but not in the literary or poetic art itself. We simply had to master another foreign language (English) and its poetic tradition from Shakespeare to the English Romantic and Victorian poets—a Romantic tradition that, be it noted, was not unfamiliar to our writers in Spanish and in our native languages—and fit the English language and its poetic tradition to our own scene and sensibility, what as individuals and as a people we had become through three centuries of Spanish rule." English, as an imposed language, was then "naturalized" or "colonized" by Filipino poets and made to reflect a native experience and an indigenous imagination.

The beginnings of Filipino poetry in English can be traced back to 1905 with the publication in Berkeley, California of *The Filipino Students' Magazine* edited by Ponciano Reyes and Jaime Araneta. This magazine contains several poems in English and in Spanish written by *pensionados* (Philippine American government scholars). During the formative period of Filipino poetry, the newspapers, magazines, and literary presses in Manila were mostly controlled by Americans who were not eager to publish poems by Filipinos. So it is ironic that the first attempts of Filipino poets writing in English would find light on the shores of the very country that was their "colonial master." The *pensionados* soon learned that the democratic ideal of freedom of speech was taken more seriously and had a wider definition in the United States than in the islands back home. In 1924 Rodolfo Dato's anthology of verse, *Filipino Poetry,* was published in Manila. Although the poems represented in that volume are not of the best quality (there is ample evidence of stilted use of language and inattention to grammar), they do portray local surroundings as only native poets can. Employing imagery learned from the poets of the English Romantic period, Filipino poets converted the skylark and the nightingale into the *kuliawan* (oriole) and the *maya* (rice bird). In his introduction to the volume, Dato refers to the poems as "the maiden songs of our native bards warbling in a borrowed language."

After only twenty-five years of colonization, one Filipino poet, Marcelo de Gracia Concepcion,[1] had eventually matured and was worthy of being recognized by the American literary establishment. This poem, "Ili-Na," is from his collection *Azucena:*

ILI-NA

And he is carried back in dreams
to the beautiful sundowns of his *ili-na.*
There is the music of young laughter.
He well remembers now his old friendships,
the long-lost ties of long ago.

There he sits under the shadows of the bells
at vesper-time.
The scenes are different now.
The voices are not the same he used to hear.

He is all alone now in the world,
for he feels strange himself.
Seemingly out of place.
Seemingly miscarried by the current of time.

He stands to go. He cannot go.
For the scent of azucena at sundown
brings back to him
the long-lost ties of long ago.

This poem shows a surprisingly modern style. The imitation of the language found in the English Romantic and Victorian periods has been dropped and the use of formal diction is minimal. Aside from the strong rhyme of "go" with "ago," Concepcion does not use any other rhymes. "Ili-Na" certainly displays the characteristics of Modern poetry in English. But is the poem worthy of inclusion in the canon of Modern American poetry? When one takes into account the history of American poetry in the 1920s when the styles, the concerns of form and meter of

English Romantic and Victorian poetry still had a strong influence on American poets, we see in "Ili-na" a breaking away from that English tradition. It is also important to note that the formalization of American free verse in the style of William Carlos Williams remained to be fully articulated until the thirties and forties. In Marcelo de Gracia Concepcion's poems we have lines of clear language and the preferred use of "plain speech." If he were given his due by the American critics of his time, can you imagine the rich textures he could have added to the Modernist movement in American poetry? But that did not happen and *Azucena* was quickly forgotten by the American literary establishment, and consequently, forgotten by the Filipinos themselves.

Another example of these early "successes" is the publication of four early poems of N.V.M. Gonzales by Harriet Monroe in the January 1934 issue of *Poetry: A Magazine of Verse:*[2]

CIRCUS SONG

I am a juggler
of hazardous moments.

My oranges are real oranges,
and I eat them all
when my show is over.

My daggers—ah,
one of them pricked the heart of
my Antonieta.

This poem shows traces of Ezra Pound's Imagist movement. From these two poems, and from looking at others in the various anthologies, we can infer that Filipinos have closely followed the development of American poetry and its poetics. From the 1940s to the present, the Filipino poet has been aware of the

Modern, New Criticism, Beat, Projectivist, New York School, Confessional, New Narrative, Multicultural, and Postmodern movements or phases of American poetry. It would be tempting to delineate the development of Filipino poetry within the same phases of its American counterparts, but that would betray the separate historical realities which occurred and influenced the writing of Filipinos. In his influential textbook *Philippine Literature: A History and Anthology,* Bienvenido Lumbera interprets the development of Filipino literature as "an alternation of assertion and acquiescence by the Filipino creative imagination" (Lumbera, IX). By responding to American literary influences in this give-and-take manner, Filipino poets gain footholds in their development of a unique poetic tradition.

The history of the Filipino poetic tradition in English can be divided into four generations: the Pioneering generation (1905-1925), which includes the poets in Rodolfo Dato's anthology *Filipino Poetry;* the Modern generation (1926-1945), which includes N.V.M. Gonzalez (1915), Alejandrino G. Hufana (1926), Dolores de Iruretagoyena de Humphrey (1919), and Manuel A. Viray (1917); the Post-War or New Critical generation (1946-1965), which includes Carlos A. Angeles (1921), Dominador I. Ilio (1913), Epifanio San Juan, Jr. (1938), and Gemino H. Abad (1939); and the Contemporary generation (1966-to present), which includes Mila D. Aguilar, Maria Luisa B. Aguilar-Cariño, Merlinda Bobis, Rofel G. Brion, Fidelito Cortes, Simeon Dumdum, Jr., Marjorie M. Evasco, Luis H. Francia, Eric Gamalinda, Fatima Lim-Wilson, Danton R. Remoto, Ricardo M. De Ungria, and Alfred Yuson.

Because the Filipino poetic tradition in English has not yet reached the hundred-year mark, these "generations" should not be taken as definite categories where a poet or series of poets would represent just one area. Some of the poets who were born in the early part of this century and who had published work in the thirties, forties, and fifties like Manuel Viray, N.V.M. Gonzales, and Alejandrino G. Hufana have continued to produce work that has grown in different stylistic and thematic directions. These generations should be taken as wide, permeable frames in which the poets' milieu, themes, and styles may indicate a certain affinity with their contemporaries, but not necessarily link them as a cohesive whole.

A separate "grouping" may be utilized for poetry written by Filipinos living in America and Filipino Americans. By mentioning a separate grouping of poets, I do not wish to imply that they have developed a poetic tradition radically different from that which developed in the Philippines. The only demarcating factor is that of geography. The writing of Filipino poets in these two continents is inextricably linked by not only the use of the English language but also by patterns of migration and immigration. In addition, many second generation Filipino American poets do not consider English a learned or foreign language but a language they have always known and grew up speaking.

The first wave of Filipino immigrants that came to the United States arrived between 1903 and 1930. They consisted mainly of male laborers who were recruited to work in the agricultural fields of Hawaii, California, and Washington and in the salmon canneries of Alaska. Along with the first wave were a small group of *pensionados* who generally came from the middle and upper classes of Filipino society and who were awarded scholarships to be "trained" in the valuable processes of democratic government, the free enterprise system, and the aesthetics of Anglo American culture in various institutions of higher learning in the United States. From these *pensionados* we find an auspicious beginning of the Filipino American tradition of poetry in English with the publication of the *Filipino Students' Magazine* in 1905 in Berkeley, California.

Included in this first wave was Jose Garcia Villa, who arrived in the United States in 1930 to subsequently earn his AB from the University of New Mexico in Albuquerque in 1933. That same year, he moved to New York City to take some courses at Columbia University and have his first and only collection of fiction, *Footnote to Youth: Tales of the Philippines and Others*, published by Charles Scribner's Sons. He then went on to publish several collections of poems that have exerted a considerable influence in the Philippines, and to a lesser extent, here in the United States: they are *Have Come, Am Here* (The Viking Press, 1942); *Volume Two* (New Directions, 1949); and *Selected Poems and New* (McDowell, Obolensky, 1958). Some Americans may remember him as the inventor of the "comma poem" or the winner of such prestigious American literary prizes as the Guggenheim Fellowship and Shelley Memorial Award.

However, the most compelling writing detailing the early immigrant experience in America would come from the laboring class in the short stories, poems, in the semi-autobiographical novel *America Is in the Heart* (1946) by Carlos Bulosan, and in *Azucena* by Marcelo de Gracia Concepcion. The issues of alienation, nostalgia for the homeland, exile, poverty, exploitation, racism, and invisibility are tackled by these pioneering writers.

In his poem "Landscape with Figures," poet Carlos Bulosan touches on the theme of alienation.

> The sun was most unkind to the place:
> history: names of men: patterns of life:
> all that the distant floodtide heaved and moved,
> breaking familiar names that immortal tongues
> clipped for the heart to cry, "Home is a foreign address,
> every step toward it is a step toward three hundred years
> of exile from the truth . . ."

In "For a Child Dying in a Tenement," Bulosan exposes the effects of poverty on an immigrant child. Note the use of the word "terror" to modify the ideal of the word "plenty." The common myth of America as "the land of plenty" becomes ironic when the author of the poem is faced with the reality of "the despair of being poor."

Dear child, you are among the first to know
the terror of plenty, the crime of innocence,
the anguish of poverty . . .
I guess I know
the cold of winter, the despair of being poor,
the terror of loneliness and of not having fun.

The second wave of Filipino immigrants arrived between 1945 and 1969. The earliest of these immigrants were the families of the more than 7,000 men who joined the Armed Forces of the United States during the Second World War. Along with this second wave came immigrants with professional and semi-professional skills which included doctors, nurses, teachers, and domestic servants. They settled in cities like San Francisco, Los Angeles, Seattle, Denver, Chicago, Detroit, Houston, Atlanta, New Orleans, Norfolk, and New York. It is the children of these immigrants that provide the first "boom" in Filipino American writing. First and second generation Filipino American writers like Jaime Jacinto, Virginia Cerenio, Serafin Syquia, Jessica Hagedorn, and Al Robles helped organize workshops, readings, and literary centers where their creative efforts could affect a presence in their communities. The locus of this "boom" was in San Francisco and the surrounding Bay Area where a beehive of literary activity occurred in the late sixties and early seventies in such organizations as the Liwanag Collective, Bay Area Pilipino American Writers, and the Kearny Street Workshop. This assertion of Filipino writing was due, in large part, to the consciousness raising and ethnic movements of the late sixties and early seventies. But, however intensely felt and well-organized this assertion of Filipino writing was in the Bay Area, it did not translate into the kinds of successes the African American, Native American, or Hispanic American writers had in the national literary venues.

The third wave, which is still in effect, began with the further relaxation of u.s. immigration policy during the late sixties. Arriving with this wave of immigrants were the "politically expatriated generation" (Campomanes p.55) who left the Philippines just before or during the fourteen years of the Marcos dictatorship, 1972-1986. The writers included are: Luis Cabalquinto, Luis Francia, Ninotchka Rosca, Epifanio San Juan, Jr., and Linda Ty-Casper. During the eighties and up to the present, several Filipino poets came to the United States to attend various creative writing programs: Maria Luisa B. Aguilar-Cariño (PhD) University of Illinois, Chicago; Fidelito Cortes (Wallace Stegner Fellowship) Stanford University; Fatima Lim-Wilson (PhD) University of Denver; Ricardo M. De Ungria (MFA) Washington University, St. Louis. After graduating, many of them went back to the Philippines to continue to publish and establish teaching careers. Some chose to stay here and put their shoulders to the American literary wheel. Among the first and second generation Filipino American poets that have received degrees in Creative Writing are: Maria Ellena Caballero-Robb (MFA) University of Michigan; Catalina Cariaga (MFA) San Francisco State University; Eugene Gloria (MFA) University of Oregon; Vince Gotera (MFA, PhD) University of Indiana, Bloomington; cyn. zarco (MFA) Columbia University.

The poems collected in this anthology are contemporary. All the poets are alive and continue to produce important work. What are the concerns of these contemporary Filipino poets?

Prevalent are themes of longing or nostalgia for the Philippines. In Rofel Brion's poem "Good Friday," he describes events in his home town: "If I were home right now / I'd be dressing up the Virgin / For this afternoon's procession." And in Luis Cabalquinto's poem "Depths of Fields," he writes: "As I look again, embraced by depths of an old / loneliness, I'm permanently returned to this world, // to the meanings it has saved for me." In Alejandrino G. Hufana's poem "From the Raw," he longs for ways of healing only found back home: "Due the hilot, faithful to my father / and before that my grandfather through to me, / I seek his malodorous, franking cures / of root mixes with lilies of the fields."

Other poems document struggles with the English language. Fatima Lim-Wilson's poem "Alphabet Soup" has the parenthetical subtitle "Mimicry as a Second Language." She finds that even the basic elements (the alphabet) of English are not sufficient to describe her state of being: "Angel of letters, feed me. / Beat your wings till I remember / Cardboard cut-outs of ABC's." In Michael Melo's poem "Unlearning English," he describes the difficult process of unlearning English in order to assimilate back into a society where Tagalog is spoken: "[Unlearning English] . . . is slow. Tedious. Like midnight mass on Christmas Eve. / The mating of tortoises. The struggle with strands / of jumbled phonics, hybrids of '*Hoy,* how are you'." In Catalina Cariaga's poem "Family Tree," she quotes one of her parents describing what would happen in class if a student spoke in a native tongue and forgot to use English: "The teachers would fine us a *centavo* each time we used / an Ilocano word."

Themes of desire and erotic encounters are also prevalent.[3] In Maria Luisa B. Aguilar-Cariño's poem "For the Lover," she assumes the voice of a French woman as she makes love to a Chinese lover: "Do this to me, / I say, do / what you do with others— / again, again— / the body at this moment / uninhabitable / except by you." In Marjorie Evasco's poem "Baked Oysters Rockefeller," she uses the dinner table at a restaurant in contemplating an erotic encounter with her lover: "Will I, I wonder, be so bold as to say / with a straight face to the waiter: we are / Carnal, you see, hungry for the Other." With the poem "Sui Veneris / The Poet of No Return," Ricardo de Ungria deftly captures the sexual act in a sustained long poem which ends with this climactic couplet: "As now uncontained she sings, fuck-fresh and profane. / And leaves me the fragrance and the stain."

An anthology of this scope has never been published in this country. Prior to my involvement with this project, I knew very little of the distinguished history of Filipino poetry written in English. This was not due to a lack of desire to acquaint myself with the subject, but rather due to the simple fact that it was

not taught or given any consideration by the English depart-
ments of the American undergraduate and graduate institutions
I attended. When I began researching this subject three years
ago, I found few books that covered Filipino literature in the
catalogs of many university and public libraries in this country.
Although there is a substantial collection of published books
(written mostly by Americans) describing the history, politics,
religions, and ethnic cultures of the Philippines, there has been
little consideration given to Filipino literature. However, the
recent publication in this country of the novels of Ninotchka
Rosca (*State of War*, 1988), Jessica Hagedorn (*Dogeaters*, 1990),
Peter Bacho (*Cebu*, 1991), and Cecilia Manguerra-Brainard
(*When the Rainbow Goddess Wept*, 1994), and of the short story
collections of Bienvenido N. Santos (*Scent of Apples*, 1979),
Marianne Villanueva (*Ginseng and Other Tales from Manila*,
1992), and N.V.M. Gonzalez (*The Bread of Salt and Other
Stories*, 1993) may indicate a second "boom" of Filipino litera-
ture in the United States.

As far as I am aware, there have been only six anthologies pub-
lished in the United States that are dedicated to the writing of
Filipinos or Filipino Americans.[4] They are: *Chorus for America: Six
Philippine Poets*, edited by Carlos Bulosan (Wagon and Star
Publishers, 1942); *New Writing from the Philippines: A Critique
and Anthology* (stories and poems) edited by Leonard Casper
(Syracuse University Press, 1966); *Philippine Writing: An Anthology*
(stories and poems) edited by T.D. Agcaoili (Greenwood Press,
1971); *Liwanag: Anthology of Filipino Writers and Artists in America*
(stories and poems) edited by the Liwanag Collective (Liwanag
Publishers, 1975); *Without Names: Poems by Bay Area Pilipino
American Writers*, edited by Shirley Ancheta, Jaime Jacinto, and
Jeff Tagami (Kearny Street Workshop Press, 1985); and the recent
*Brown River, White Ocean: An Anthology of Twentieth-Century
Philippine Literature in English* (stories and poems) edited by Luis
H. Francia (Rutgers University Press, 1993). Except for *Brown
River, White Ocean,* most of these anthologies have long been out

of print and are difficult to locate. In a very real way they have been "lost" or "forgotten." In using these terms I take into account the polemics of "historical amnesia" and of "invisibility" which has been applied to the Filipino condition in its relation to the experience of American colonization and neocolonization. As the Filipino critic Oscar V. Campomanes points out: "The invisibility of the Philippines became a necessary historiographical phenomenon because the annexation of the Philippines proved to be constitutionally and culturally problematic for American political and civil society around the turn of the century and thereafter." Thus, as the consequence of American colonization and because of America's "invisibility" to its own imperialistic acts in the Philippines, the Filipino writer has been burdened with the label of being "forgotten."

In her introduction to the ground-breaking anthology of Asian American fiction *Charlie Chan Is Dead* (Penguin Books, 1993), Jessica Hagedorn states a personal reason for creating the book: "This is an anthology I created for selfish reasons; a book I wanted to read that had never been available to me." The poems and poets represented in *Returning a Borrowed Tongue* are really parts of ourselves that have been denied, lost, hidden, or forgotten. To many, this book may serve as a (re)discovery of a notable poetic tradition. It should also signify a (re)beginning that will propel the Filipino poet well into the next century. In the early period of tutelage, Filipino poets borrowed a foreign tongue to express their poetic voices. Today, with this anthology of poems written in English, we return this borrowed tongue.

I would like to thank Allan Kornblum and the wonderful staff at Coffee House Press for believing in this anthology. Also to the following editors and individuals who helped point me to more Filipino poets: Inez Baranay, Naomi Shihab Nye, Howard Junker, and Jeffrey McDaniel. To the Corporation of Yaddo for support and encouragement. To Jimmy Abad, Luis Francia, N.V.M. Gonzalez, Jean Gier, Eric Gamalinda, Maneng Viray, Sonny San Juan, Jr., and all the poets in this anthology, my deepest gratitude. And, finally, to my parents Alfonso and Sophie and to my wife Denise who have made it all possible.

FOOTNOTES

[1]It is interesting to note what the American publisher thought of this book. The following is a quote from its own blurb: "*Azucena* is, as far as its publishers are aware, the first volume of English poetry to be written by a Philippine poet, and this fact alone would make the appearance of the book notable. . . . The words are those of a Western land but the accent and the sentiment come to us from the East" (Abad, *Man of Earth,* 323).

[2]I quote the anecdote provided by N.V.M. Gonzalez concerning this event: "One day the ferry boat came with my copy of *Poetry: A Magazine of Verse*—perhaps the first to ever reach Calapan. In fact there was no one with whom I could share my joy. I was nineteen and had actually sold my first poems. No one in town, for that matter, could honor Harriet Monroe's check for twelve dollars" (Abad, *Man of Earth,* 322).

[3]It is important to note that the Philippines has long been dominated by the Catholic Church and its ideals of morality. Consequently, the publication of erotic literature, especially by women, carries with it the burden of being ostracized by society. Sexual expression through any public medium is such a taboo in Filipino society that even the Tagalog word for "sex" does not appear in most local dictionaries. Noel Mateo's poem in this anthology, "There Is No Word for Sex in Tagalog," illustrates the effects of this prudish behavior.

[4]In the Philippines there has been a strong tradition of publishing Filipino poetry in English in individual collections and in anthologies. It is useful to mention that the first of these anthologies was *Filipino Poetry,* edited by Rodolfo Dato (J.S. Agustin and Sons, Manila, 1924). Other important anthologies of Filipino poetry are: *Heart of the Island: An Anthology of Philippine Poetry in English,* edited by Manuel A. Viray (University Publishing Co., Manila, 1947); *Philippine Poetry Annual 1947-1949,* edited by Manuel A. Viray (Barangay Press Book, Manila, 1950); *A Doveglion Book of Philippine Poetry: From Its Beginnings to the Present (1910*

to 1962), edited by Jose Garcia Villa (Lyd Arguilla-Salas and Alberto S. Florentino, Manila, 1962); and the recent *A Native Clearing,* edited by Gemino Abad (University of the Philippines Press, Quezon City, 1993).

WORKS CITED

Abad, Gemino H., and Edna Z. Manlapaz, ed. *Man of Earth: An Anthology of Filipino Poetry and Verse from English: 1905 to the Mid-'50s.* Manila: Ateneo de Manila University Press, 1989.

———, "Towards a 'Poetic' History of Filipinas: The Theme of the Lost Country." *Journal of English Studies I* (December, 1993): 1-14.

Campomanes, Oscar V. "Filipinos in the United States." *Reading the Literatures of Asian America.* Ed. Shirley Geok-lin Lim and Amy Ling. Philadelphia: Temple University Press, 1992.

Lumbera, Bienvenido, and Cynthia Nograles Lumbera, ed. *Philippine Literature: A History and Anthology.* Manila: National Book Store Inc., 1982.

RETURNING A BORROWED TONGUE

GEMINO H. ABAD

The Light in One's Blood

To seek our way of thinking
by which our country is found,
I know but do not know,
for its language too is lost.
To find our trail up a mountain
without a spirit guide—
here is no space where words in use
might stake a claim.

Speaking is fraught with other speech.
Through all our fathers, Spain
and America had invented our souls
and wrought our land and history.
How shall I think counter to the thick
originating grain of their thought?
"I have not made or accepted
their words. My voice holds them at bay."

Look then without words,
nor jump about like ticks
missing their dumb meat.
If there be enough blood yet
in our story for counterpoise,
in speech take no meaning
from elsewhere,
be more thorough that passion.

Whence does one come
when he speaks, his eyes lighting up?
Before speech, all words are dead,

their legends blind.
No one comes from language,
the truth is what words dream.
One speaks, and language comes,
the light in one's blood.

What ravening lions roar
in our blood for our thoughts?
We too have our own thunder
from lost insurrections;
even the present seems a gift,
but mostly unopened.
So much thought is scattered
like grain upon burnt ground.

The soil is ours, and inters
the secret bones of our loss.
We must know our loss, all things
that ghost our time.
Speak now, collect every bone,
lay the pieces together.
Here is true speaking—
a mountain rises beneath our feet!

Is language already given?
—yet we have its use:
a double forgery!
No essences are fixed by words.
Proceed by evacuation
of first seeing; in emptiness
gather the pieces
of breaking light.

No language is beforehand
but its shadow; there's nothing

4

in the script, but the other's myth
that now frets your soul.
What breathed there before the words
took their hue and creed?
How, with the same words,
shall another tale be told?

The same words, but not the given,
for void its speech of empire!
Our eyes must claim their right
to our landscape and its names.
What cataract of other minds
has flooded their sight?
We must even fall from our own sky
to find our earth again.

Jeepney

Consider honestly
this piece of storm
in our city's entrails.
Incarnation of scrap,
what genius of salvage!
Its crib now molds our space,
its lust gewgaws our sight.

In rut and in flood,
claptrap sex of traffic,
jukebox of hubbub—
I mark your pride of zigzag
heeds no one's limbs nor light.

I sense our truth laughing
in our guts, I need
no words to fix its text.

This humdrum phoenix in our street
is no enigma.
It is a daily lesson of history
sweating in a tight corner.
Its breakdowns and survivals
compose our Book of Revelation.
It may be the presumptive engine
of our last mythology.

Look, our Macho Incarnate,
sweat towel hung around his neck.
He collects us where the weathers
of our feet strand us.
His household gods travel with him,
with the Virgin of Sudden Mercy.
Our Collective Memory, he forgets
no one's fare. Nor anyone's destiny.

See how our countrymen cling
to this trapeze against all hazards.
All our lives we shall be acrobats
and patiently survive.
Our bodies feed on proximity,
our minds rev up on gossip.
We flock in small spaces,
and twitter a country of patience.

Here is our heartland still.
When it dreams of people,
it returns empty to itself,
having no power of abstraction.

6

Abandoned to itself
and in no one's care,
Jeepneys caroom through it,
our long country of patience.

Nights I lie awake, I hear
a far-off tectonic rumble.
Is it a figment of desolation
from that reliquary of havoc,
or, out of its dusty hardiwood,
that obduracy of mere survival,
a slow hoard of thunder
from underground spirit of endurance?

Toys

Now our boys have such toys
as my brother and I never dreamed;
Did the same spirit stir our make-believe?
Yet outdoors was where we took its measure.

But how could I wish it were otherwise
from them, and would it be wise
since other kids the same quarry inhabit
where X-men rage their fantastic war?

Indeed we knew the hot spill of blood,
with slingshots searched the bushes and trees,
but also knew ourselves pierced
where the world's songs first were made.

But those video games, or toys perhaps
have changed their meaning.
In the overflood of their kind,
they've lost their round of seasons.

It may be the same with the world's
weather, but in our time,
there was one season for kites
when the wind seemed to make the sky
          rounder;

There was another, for marbles and rubber
          bands,
the earth firmer, the blaze of sunshine
          brighter;
and yet another, for tops and wheels,
as streetwise we vied for dusty prizes.

          And when the rains came,
and the skies fell with the thunderclap,
how we would run in drenched nakedness
to dare a lightning race to the edge of time.

But how shall I travel to my boys' hearts
and break their dreadnought of heroes,
and find, as when light breaks,
the pieces of their manhood whole?

O, their heroes create them,
but if they could invent their games
and stage their future, might they not
surprise their hero with their fate?

Holy Order

Our words do not lie apart,
One from the other, like monads,
But dwell peaceably together
Like a congregation of monks.

They follow strictly
The Rules of their Order,
And keep all the holy hours
By bell and candle and book.

Unearthly their vocation—
Who called, who are chosen,
No one knows, but outside,
The demons of change howl and gnash
        their teeth.

And so secluded, so scheduled,
They are set apart,
Our world unawares their altar,
Our thoughts and passions their weather.

Would you know what they worship
Or what their prayers lift?
Their meditations most strangely *shape*
Our daily speech.

At night their incense drifts
Into your dreams with primeval memories,
But never shall your hands swing
In trance their golden censers.

You never see their faces,

Their cowls hide their eyes.
They listen attentively to homilies
Only from their breed.

Their sandals leave no trace
Of their comings and goings;
Their feet are their most holy parts.

O, but when they sing in choir,
You shall be quite unhinged,
For their scripture, if you listen,
Is what you glimpse but never hold.

GEMINO H. ABAD's collections of poetry are *Fugitive Emphasis* (1973), *In Another Light* (1976), *The Space Between* (1985), and *Poems and Parables* (1988). He is also the coeditor of the influential anthologies of Filipino poetry *Man of Earth* and *A Native Clearing*. He is an associate for poetry in the University of the Philippines Creative Writing Center and a co-founder of the Philippines Literary Arts Council.

KARINA AFRICA-BOLASCO

Sauna 2

I choose to come every noon
when I have the room all to myself.
Then I dare be fully bare.
I stretch out on the planks
and from their gaps heat spurts.
Making my flesh tingle
in all the special places.
My fingers tread lines of sweat
and catch pores popping.
I touch myself
as no one ever would:
the unders, the beneaths,
the tops, the beyonds,
and the inbetweens.
All at once I feel your mouth,
like the heat all over me.
Powerful hands cup my curves,
or whatever remains of them.
The searching legs lock mine.
The body, the heart,
smarting from unimagined wounds,
almost cringe
from imagined pleasure.
I pat my buttocks:
once, thrice.

It's just the heat.

KARINA AFRICA-BOLASCO is the Publishing Manager of Anvil Publishing, Inc.
in the Philippines. Her poems have appeared in the *Diliman Review* and *Ani.*

CARLOS A. ANGELES

Words

I.
All the time I was talking as if you listened.

To hear these words spoken in a coil of tongues.
These words that spool off from eddies of fluxing
winds, the cruxes of water in air involute.

In minor hands these words construct assemblage
from inferior earth amphoras to hold in water
sprung from a weight of hidden springs.

II.
All day burning letters of exquisite speeches.

Oratorios in a chaos of tongues lift from the fire
of their being, like the resolute anguish
of lost souls in the purging cells in hereafter.

And cellos and bassoons in discordance repeat
words that I speak, their dark syllables repeating
a spoilage of echoes in the void. Muted. Unheard.

Light Invested

The dark which canopies the dawning skies.
To be ripped in a flood of morning light.

This brittle startle which seals and reaps the eyes'
Slept wonders. Core of the sky's most intense.

This sun that bowers pure beneficence.
Whose living heat pours out in silence stark

As in the scattered morning flight of larks
Who shadow silence in their skyward thrust;

As in the silent scrawls of light abrupt
That stricken thunders in the dark of night.

CARLOS A. ANGELES is a Palanca Memorial awardee, and winner of the Republic Cultural Heritage Award in 1964 for his collection of poetry *A Stun of Jewels*. He lives in La Puente, California.

MILA D. AGUILAR

Pall Hanging over Manila

As the boat glides slowly
portward
carrying the fresh winds
from sea and countryside
one can see the pall hanging over Manila,
city of one's birth,
one's most fevered child.
The dissonance of cars bustling to and fro
greets ears used to the silence of cicadas
chirping warmly from cool treetops—
and later the grey smirking faces lined up
in jeeps reeking of sweat
and soot-laden collars.

Oh the pall that hangs over Manila,
city of my birth to violence,
my most fevered child!
On a hilltop at night
far from the smokestacks belching
the daily black of exploitation
I watch her, bejeweled now
with varicolored gems of light
moving, seeming slow from a distance.
She lies
hard black stone inlaid
with clusters of gold and diamonds and rubies,
hiding the many sins lurking behind
esteros and seedy bars,
knowing yet not thinking
of the unfathomable grief she causes,

14

grief causing lonely acts
pushing onward
a hungry desperate people.

Manila: metropolis mushrooming
not out of any dream
but the sweat of millions
on steel-hot machines
and the toil of millions more
on placid-fertile greens.

Poem from Sierra Madre

"Nature is on the side of the fighting masses.
Command every inch of it with genius."
-Jose Maria Sison

The rains have come
warriors beloved of the people,
it is time to avenge Crispin Tagamolila.
The forest, swathed now by the dark of the sky,
has become even more impervious
to the frantic roar of helicopters;
If they come we shall in any case
shoot panic into their dragonfly wings.
Let the enemy commandos
trudge up the Sierra Madre
with their six-pound packs.
The mud that will gather on their boots
shall add to the weight on their backs.
We for our part
shall slide nimbly down

the mountain trails,
lightly up the giant boulders:
we serve the people,
the people are with us.
Today, as our comrades below
help plant the season's new seedlings,
we shall run the enemy down:
the flash floods will take them,
the flash floods of our anger
will bloodily take them.

MILA D. AGUILAR's collection of poetry, *A Comrade Is as Precious as a Rice Seedling*, was published by Kitchen Table: Women of Color Press in 1987. On August 6, 1984, she was jailed by agents of the Marcos dictatorship on charges of "subversion and conspiracy to commit rebellion," subsequently spending a year and a half in jail until her release was ordered by President Corazon Aquino on February 27, 1986.

MARIA LUISA B. AGUILAR-CARIÑO

For the Lover

Nothing has changed, it is the same
as it was before.
                    -Marguerite Duras

I. CROSSING THE RIVER
The ferry drags
its coarse weight
through coffee-colored
water, waves of heat.
Fowls clamor
at the hiss of penned
reptiles.

I stand apart
on the platform,
under the dusky rose
cloud of my fedora.
Slowly the mangroves
recede. A moist wind slips
up my frayed shift.

Leaning over,
I see my face, its creased
reflection, the amber
light impaled
in a bauble on my high-
heeled shoe.

II. IN THE CHINESE QUARTER
These bones, my body,

ignite by touch
and glance.
The bronze walls
of our skin shudder,
contract.
Dark oils perfume
the air, whetting
hunger.

Against the floor's tiled
arabesques and palmettoes
we devour each other,
pant through floodlit
hollows of flesh.

Do this to me,
I say, do
what you do with others—
again, again—
the body at this moment
uninhabitable
except by you.

III. TROMPE L'OEIL
No one, nothing
forced me into this—
not the brother
in whose shadow
all of us were outcast, not
the mother lost
to herself in the house
at Sadec, not even
the little brother who danced
with me and wept for me.

18

Already my fingers uncurl,
beckoning
to a fate beyond the dark
outline of your head
pressed close
upon my belly.
Past the latticed screen,
the voices rising
and falling,
calling out for plums,
bamboo shoots, willow
baskets—
it is market day.

IV. BILLET-DOUX
If I willed it, I know
you would consume yourself
for me, feed on nothing
but shadows, opium.

V. NIGHT MUSIC
Across the water
in the blue villa
the angry father will tear
his goatee to shreds,
scattering joss sticks
and curses.

Because of this
I hurt you, saying,
"All of this meant
nothing."
I behave

as if I had
no shame.

A bowl of fruit,
an inkwell sending forth
the odor of leaves
and creotonne—even
the grey cat quietly
regarding me
with onyx eyes
as I write—
will someday seem
terrible
as the night
swirling the clear
notes of a waltz,
delivering me
at last
to this
knowledge.

Gabi

I.
Three sunrises
distant, at the river's
lip, the women unwrap
their heads
from many-times-
starched bandannas.

In the shimmering
heat, pleats
of hair unloose
a fortnight's rain
of dust, lice-eggs—

and the fair one
steps, body
beaconing wind,
into the stunned
shallows.

Take heed, say the women.
Never bathe
by moonlight. Fasten
your shutters, burn
votive candles—
around your neck,
string scapulars.

Trailing a spasm
of fish, moth wings
and beggar's ticks,
the river god breaks
through the wet
underworld of dreams.

Now her feet swell,
they grow
heavy and waterlogged,
the green sap rising
to her eyes.

II.
Tonight we'll sup
on fairy tales:
a dish of boiled
gabi, whose leaves resemble
blue-green hearts
fed on rain, on waters
of darkest jealousy;
plumes of the red *labuyo,*
ginger roots that once
were nuggets of gold.

Departing
from the story,
I invent
no refusals. Look
how lovingly I watch
you shape each
spoonful to your mouth,
each piece steamed
to translucence. Later,
the paroxysms of warmth,
the foreknowledges
of taste.

Dinakdakan

For Mama Tet

This could be
the supermarket of your dreams,
the shelves slick and
showy with fruit, wide-

mouthed mason jars of herring,
rice grains longer
than your fingernail.

Our shopping cart would quickly swell
with breads whose names till now
were fable: rye, stone-ground
wheat, poppyseed buns;
the brie and Camembert
longed for at Christmas time
instead of the yearly *queso
de bola;* the Spam and corned
beef worth a whole week's pay.

And then I think of you
as on a trip to market long ago:
the marvel was not merely
how the wind lifted our hair,
knifed raw the flesh of our mouths,
wrists, cheeks—how our rubber
boots were worthless in steady rain
and slippery mud.

It was you, plunging a bare
arm into a pail of still-breathing milkfish,
certain which had the sweetest belly;
knowing where to find
tamarind pods cracking
out of their rinds for ripeness,
the lemon grass for boiling
with white rice, the river snails
to steep into a heady broth.
(We extricated these with safety
pins, smacking lips, fingers.)

Among the rows of plastic-sealed,
aseptically packaged food,
I stare and stare, imagining flat,
dried, salted fish-shapes pressed
between the cereal boxes,
fresh blood and entrails forming
a dark pool on the white linoleum.

(Above the click and hum
of computerized cash registers
I hear your singing knife
slice pigs' ears paper-thin,
your fork twirl thick
with clouds of boiled brain and minced
shallots for the evening meal.

Familiar

Like someone newly dead
I'm mourned on my seventh
birthday. Nose and forehead stamped
with blood, I wander into the house
after a fall among the spiked flower
beds, rousing the womenfolk
to keening.

Poultices of warm vinegar. Years,
rows of crooked teeth later,
my face becomes familiar.
Once frail, my limbs
have filled out from balls of fish

24

and sticky rice my aunts
fed me with their fingers.

They tell me I am not beautiful,
but that my eyes are clear.
I drink from a clay bowl:
a forest of green mussel
shells floats, opening
to reveal mother-
of-pearl insides.

In the evenings my ears fold
close, against the clatter of dishes,
the sing-song of voices
bordering the road. I murmur
these incantations, spell words
on blue-lined paper: *bizarre, irrevocable,*
reproach, syllable, steerage, ballast,
gesture—taking them with me to sleep
like furry animals, hiding them
in my mouth like pebbles
newly dug up from the moonlit
garden—taste of earth,
crushed bones, verbena, flared
nasturtiums.

MARIA LUISA B. AGUILAR-CARIÑO is currently a Fulbright Fellow in the
PhD program at the University of Illinois at Chicago. She won the Manila
Critics' Circle National Book Award in 1993 for her collection of poetry
Cartography and Other Poems on Baguio. Her poems appear in U.S. journals
such as *Black Warrior Review, Folio, Journal of American Culture,* and *Bomb.*

NERISSA S. BALCE

Pizza and Pretense

We are ravenous after our
encounters. And so we
visit the pizza place that
makes 'em the way you like 'em, hot
and crunchy with extra spices and cheese.
Propriety demands we hide
conspicuous marks made by impassioned
lips and teeth. So we dress
our best, covering our bodies
warm and wet only hours ago.
My hair still damp,
we both smell of sweet soap.
You look scrubbed to a perfect pink
like an altar boy.

There is a lipstick smudge
on your left shirtsleeve.
There is a pink mark on
my nape. I feel the folds of fat on my
belly while I imagine
the taste of melted cheese
on crust. I study your
hands now on the table,
properly clasped the way we pray
at Mass.

NERISSA S. BALCE taught literature at De La Salle University where she received an MA in Philippine Studies. She is presently a PhD candidate in English at the University of California, Berkeley.

JOANN BALINGIT

Quiet Evening, Home Away

Coffee turned cold in the pot.
I photographed you
painting.
Watched the incense burn.

Camel alone
on the coffee tray.

What was that
noise in the window,
a noise like breathing,
not the radio—could a giant
stork be out there
gliding in the dark?

Her empty nest
atop the cypress tree.

Silk veil—full of grace,
rise from the tiled floor!

There is only one heaven,
She has swept it under her wings.
Watch how she
unfolds them.

In the name of the fire,
the earth and all rooftop antennae:
listen to the wind
reciting the leaves.

The moon is sipping dawn. Vast armies
of bread boards jostle in the alleys,
and next door the leather boys
up already pounding.

Said the Fog to the Mosque
at last: let me take your hand.
In the moonlight, my silk
will sharpen your hooves.

But for now. To practice
reasons for this trip:
Follow a mosquito
across the lamplit room.

JoAnn Balingit won an Artist's Fellowship in Literature from the Delaware Arts Council in 1994. She lives in Newark, Delaware where she coedits the poetry magazine *Blades*.

MERLINDA BOBIS

Word Gifts for an Australian Critic

I bring you words freshly
pried loose from between my wishbone.

Mahal, oyayi, halakhak, lungot, alaala.

Mate those lips,
then heave a wave in the throat,
and lull the tip of the tongue
at the roof of the mouth.
Mahal, mahal, mahal.
"Love, love, love"—let me,
in my tongue.

Then I'll sing you a tale.
Oyaiiyaiiyayii, oyayi, oyayi.
Once, mother pushed the hammock
away—*oyaiiyaiiyayii,*
the birthstrings severed from her wrist
when I married
an Australian.

So now, I can laugh with you.
Halakhak! How strange.
Your kookaburras roost in my windpipe
when I say, "laughter!"
as if feathering a new word.
Halakhak-k-k-k-kookaburra!

But if suddenly you pucker
the lips—*lung*—

as if you were about to break
into tears or song—watch out,
the splinter cuts too far too much—*lunggggggg*—
unless withdrawn—*kot*—
in time. *Lungkot.*
Such is our word for "sadness."

Ah! For relief, release, wonder or peace
in any tongue. "Ah!"
of the many timbres,
this is how remembering begins—*ah!*—
and is repeated—*lah!-ah!-lah!*
Alaala. This is our word for "memory."

How it forks
like a wishbone.

Mahal, oyayi, halakhak, lungkot, alaala.

How they flow
East-West-East-West-East
in one bone of two marrows.
Forget dichotomy.
I need not break me
for a wish.

Driving to Katoomba

Today, you span the far mountains
with an arm and say,
"This I offer you—

all this blue sweat
of eucalypt."

Then you teach me
how to startle kookaburras
in my throat,
and point out to me orion
among the glowworms.

I, too, can love you
in my dialect, you know,
punctuated with cicadas
and their eternal afternoons:

Mahal kita. Mahal kita.

I can even save you monsoons,
pomelo-scented bucketfuls
to wash your hair with.

And for want of pearls,
I can string you the whitest seeds
of green papayas,

then hope that, wrist to wrist,
we might believe again
the single rhythm passing
between pulses,

even when pearls
become the glazed-white eyes
of a Bosnian child
caught in the cross-fire,

or when monsoons cannot wash

the trigger-finger clean
in East Timor,

and when Tibetans
wrap their dialect
around them like a robe,

lest orion grazes them
from a muzzle.

Yes, even when among the Sinhalese
the birds mistake the throat
for a tomb

as gun smoke lifts
from the Tamil mountains,

my tongue will still unpetrify
to say,

Mahal Kita. Mahal Kita.

MERLINDA BOBIS has published three collections of poetry: *Rituals, Ang Lipad Ay Awit Sa Apat Na Hangin* (in Tagalog), and *Cantata of the Warrior Woman/Kantada ng Babaing Mandirigma Daragang Magayon,* an epic poem in two versions: Tagalog and English. Inspired by the native tradition of epic chanting, she has performed her poems in the Philippines, Australia, France, and China. She currently lectures on the Faculty of Creative Arts, University of Wollongong, Australia.

ROFEL G. BRION

Love Song

One long and humid afternoon
While we were having truth
Justice, fidelity and chastity
Over tall glasses of iced tea,
You lazily bit into your biscuit
And casually mentioned
How once, in a crowded jeepney,
Your child wailed from hunger
So you quickly bared your breast
To feed her.
              When you began
To defend your thesis
That ordinary people in ordinary jeepneys
Remain cool and composed
At the sight of bare breasts
As long as they are a mother's
Wanting to feed her child,
I bit the rim of my glass
As I tried to decide
Whether I wished I were
A stranger in that jeepney
Or the father of your child.

One Morning beside a Pond

"I never thought frogs
Ate their young," she said
As he pried open its mouth
And shoved in some tadpoles.

"I never thought so
Either," he answered
As she gently stroked
Its quivering throat.
"I think it would like
Some more," she said
As she watched its eyes
Very quickly roll.

"All right, then, whatever
You say," he answered
As she tightly gripped
Its stiffening legs.

"It has had enough
It seems," she said
And he dropped the frog
Into the cold, clear pond.

"All right now, come on
And play," he answered
As he held her wrist
And led her into the woods.

Good Friday

If I were home right now
I'd be dressing up the Virgin
For this afternoon's procession.

This morning
I'd have taken out the body of wood
From the storeroom (it had stood there
For the year, with old clothes and toys
And Grandmother's deathbed),
Father and I would have put it
On top of a small table
In the middle of the living room
While Mother spread on the sofa
The long black veil, the white gown,
The silver crown and a heart with seven daggers,
The golden, curly, long hair.
The hands and head of ivory
And four drops of crystal tears
(Glued to her cheeks for Good Friday,
Very carefully peeled off for Easter Sunday).

While my nephews and nieces
Watch me in great anticipation,
And sweat glues my shirt to my skin,
I dress up the body of wood,
Give it hands, a head, a veil,
A crown, a heart, some tears,
Making it grieve for the yearly death
Of its only begotten son.
(Two dawns later,
She will be made to rejoice
As she meets this same son

To the songs of my winged nieces).
But now, thousands of miles away from home,
From my parents, my sister, my nephews and nieces,
I shiver in the cold beside the fireplace
While I watch in great anticipation
These fine drops of snow,
Tears falling, glueing themselves
To the window of my small room.

If Fortune Smiles

If fortune smiles,
You will see her
Tonight.

Wait for her under
The acacia tree.
Time it so that
The first star
Is about to rise
And the first dry leaf
Is about to fall
From the longest branch
Of the acacia tree.

When all is set
Shut your eyes,
Wait for the blowing
Of the lukewarm breeze.
It just might
Be her breath.

Do not open your eyes.
Wait for the breeze
To cool down a bit
Until your eyelids
Moisten a little.
Let yourself be sleepy,
Or doze off a bit,
Or fall into deep slumber.

You will be awakened
By the touch of her lips
On your parched lips.

Then she will
Take you by your hand.
She will bring you
To the longest branch
Of the acacia tree,
And together you will pluck
The first dry leaf
Which is yet to fall,
And together you will offer it
To the first star
Which is yet to rise,

If fortune smiles on you
Tonight.

ROFEL G. BRION teaches at the Ateneo de Manila University and is the director of its Interdisciplinary Studies Program. His first book of poetry, *Baka Sakali (Maybe by Chance),* won the Manila Critics' Circle National Book Award for poetry in 1990. Among his other awards are a British Council Grant in 1986, a Residency Fellowship at the Hawthornden Castle in Scotland, and a Fulbright Fellowship in 1991.

MARIA ELENA CABALLERO-ROBB

Memoranda for Rosario

Since I am "the bookish," just like you, *abuelita,*
since it skips a generation and I've missed you, I'll tell you
I read a story today about a man who rushes
to the hospital bed of his dying friend
only to find she's already dead. He has missed her,
but the thing is, when he walks in
he doesn't realize yet—the monitors have just been disconnected
and trolleyed off, the doctor and an orderly are down the hall
at the nurse's station making the call. And he wants
so much for her to be alive,
so he can say good-bye, say something worthy—
that he dashes over at the sight of her, even though already
her skin is going grey and plasticky, and lifts her
by the armpits to hold her, as if he were the one person in the world
in whose arms she ought to die.
                                                        That's the kind of fool
I am sometimes, hoping to find the meat
of drama in events from which I am removed
in the most pedestrian ways: it was years ago
and I just wasn't there, not even thought of yet.
The kind of fool I was, my last chance dribbled away
on *no time, no money* flying into Manila
three days late, in time to hold hands with aunts and cousins,
a chain of women in front of the casket droning, *Holy Mary*
pray for us, sinners,
                                        now and at the hour of our death.
I moved my lips silently for the parts I had forgotten,
out of practice, and afterward complaining about America
with a thicket of cousins in black dresses, I stole
my first glance at your face

                    the possibility of the awkward looks
we might have exchanged chalked over, I knew,
        first by cataracts and now this.
I kept thinking about the word *untimely,*
        wondering which one of us it described best.

That night my mother and I slept in the same bed,
first time since I was very small, in the mansion
of our elderly cousin, a corrupt governor in Rizal.
And I congratulated myself on being there, for once,
when she sat bolt upright in the dark screaming—baying at a vision
of you, I assumed, though she wouldn't say. I held her
like a daughter accustomed to holding her mother and soothing,
I'm here. It's all right, I'm here.
                    As if I were familiar
with the architecture of that nightmare, could help her negotiate
turns I'd seen her take a million times. I pretended
it was possible to be present, to bear witness.

But why am I telling you this?
    It must be the flicker
    of comfort this little conjuring act affords.

Abracadabra—
        as if I expect some kind of redemption
from resurrecting you, bleating
        out of the blankish wilds
of space, as if you possessed an antidote,
    a curing specter who'd save us
if we could just make you give up your secrets.

Like drowsy kids shocked to be awake,
    we're running our hands all over our bodies,
looking for the something
we lost back there, the organ
        cut out in our sleep.

As for you, I confess, there's no real puzzlement,
no wondering where you are now. I don't need
    a map to that world you're in,
because the fact is, it's always too late.

There's just this meandering, my attempt to construct

something grand out of simple mis-timing—
                    not the answers, but the baroque lack of them,
            the crack, the missing thing
become elaborate.

Dear Rosario

> *I determined to devote my entire life to [God's] service & desired*
> *that all might taste of the stream of living water from which I cooled*
> *my thirst. But the world allured me & in an unguarded moment I*
> *listened to her siren voice.*
> —*Emily Dickinson, Letters, 28 March, 1846*

Why don't you shock the whole town and ride down
Main Street on a bicycle, dressed like a man?
Because the nuns will peep into your classroom
like magpies darting after trinkets. A diamond in gold winks
on your ring finger, but your husband's a guerilla.
He's left you to help the GIs
fight the Japanese in the mountains.

Put down, please, the papers you are marking.
Unclasp your hands, twist off the wedding
ring scorching your finger. Its metal's oxidizing
anyway, burning off atom by atom,

40

like every other thing in the world—evaporating
like a husband.
                              Grandmother-across-the-water,
before we were even probable you knew faith
as inflammation. The Sacred Heart encircled
by its crown of thorns stood out from Christ's body,
too literal, grotesque. He had opened his chest cavity
like a tabernacle he was admitting you with outstretched palms
and eyes rolled heavenward—and at the sight
you grew expansive.
                              We are fine,
though it is very cold here, and the sun
in the sky is so weak the fog
does not burn off for hours. When we were small
we learned faith was tongues of flame, once,
standing up in gaudy plumes over the apostles' heads.
But the soul's not quite so tactless anymore,
and we speak only one language here, the others are verboten.
Though, God-fed, you've become a giantess
we are shrivelled here and the waters, wide between you and us.
We know He won't shrink oceans to crossable ponds
just to match the length of your stride.

Grandfather was the projectionist in the Naga City movie house
where the beautiful girl in her round glass cage
took your pesos and reeled off the pink cardboard tickets,
where the velvet seats were fire engine red—redder
than the underskin of the eyes of women saints,
whom faith inflamed to weeping, fueled by visions.
Who's to say which blush exceeded the other in ardor?
The affair was mirthless, as though it were Man's duty,
and babies came—his but not yours—quick
and by surprise like a string of miracles.

                    In the north
the mud slides extinguished platoons of souls,
and in Baguio City the women lit votives in the church.
But not for him—though he became a hero,
and lived to tell about it.
If you were afire with the flame of the spirit
I can't believe the monsoons didn't snuff it out.
When the streets flooded, you folded
four children into the bureau drawers
to sleep like mice in a fairy story.
When he never came home, you could have waded
through waist-deep waters, and let
a sweet new current overmaster you.

For you, there was only one permissible romance:
to be fed from the mouth of the Paraclete,
to grow great with spirit and never give birth.
A husband who is a cornerstone, a husband
to slake the spirit, who hears
what no one else can hear
because it is unspeakable.

MARIA ELENA CABALLERO-ROBB received her MFA in Creative Writing from the University of Michigan. Her poems appear in *Antioch Review, Indiana Review, Passages North,* and *Hyper Age.* She has received residency fellowships to the MacDowell Colony and the Ragdale Foundation.

LUIS CABALQUINTO

Depths of Fields

I walk some hundred paces from the old house
where I was raised, where many are absent now,

and the rice fields sweep into view: there where
during home leaves I'm drawn to watch on evenings

such as this, when the moon is fat and much given
to the free spending of its rich cache of light

which transmutes all things: it changes me now,
like someone restored to the newness of his life.

Note the wind's shuffle in the crown of tall coconut
trees; the broad patches of moon-flecked water—

freshly-rowed with seedlings; the grass huts of
croppers, windows framed by the flicker of kerosene

lamps: an unearthly calm pervades all that is seen.
Beauty unreserved holds down a country's suffering.

Disclosed in this high-pitched hour: a long-held
secret displayed by ambition and need, a country

boy's pained enchantment with his hometown lands
that remains intact in a lifetime of wanderings.

As I look again, embraced by depths of an old
loneliness, I'm permanently returned to this world,

to the meanings it has saved for me. If I die now,
in the grasp of childhood fields, I'll miss nothing.

The Value Added in Smashing a German Roach on the Bathroom Door

Parked in the office john, going
        to be free of the body's
detritus, a day's accumulation,
        I chance upon this brown German
roach pulling its fat body
        across the bathroom door,
an eggcase sticking half out
        of its butt. I seize
the annual report copy off the tank
        and—yes—swiftly perform
two feats of solid extermination
        in a single sitting! I
rise, grin at the quick stock split
        of an early morning's pleasure.

The Ordinance

Stepping out of my apartment building,
One early morning, I meet a poem
Being walked around the block by its master.

44

I follow them.

At the corner, the poem stops and bends its hind legs.
Something drops to the pavement.
Another poem?

I quicken my steps.

But before I can reach the dropped object
The poem master notices it.
He turns back and takes out a poem scooper.

In one sweep he scoops up the new poem.

He sees me coming and hurriedly
Slips the scooped poem into a pouch,
Then wipes the pavement clean.

Keeping an eye on his poems, the poem master moves away.

Later, at the newsstand, I pick up the paper
And learn what this is all about:
A new ordinance passed, banning poems from littering the streets—

To promote public hygiene and better relations among the citizens.

LUIS CABALQUINTO is the author of *The Dogeater and Other Poems*
(1989), *The Ibalon Collection* (1991), and *Dreamwanderers* (1992).
His poems are widely published in the U.S., Australia, and Europe
and he divides his time between Magarao, his hometown in Bikol
in the Philippines, and New York City.

An Afternoon in Pangasinan with No Electricity

In the yellow of butter
My mother colors my skin
In the yellow of sun
My skin becomes brown
In the yellow of yolk
My grandfather finds an egg
In the yellow of noon
We eat the baby chick
Balot, they call it
"Long life!" he says
And discards the purple shell

Check One

The government asks me to "check one" if I want money.
I just laugh in their faces and say
"How can you ask me to be one race?"

I stand proudly before you, a proud Filipino
who knows how to belt hard-gospel songs
played to African drums at a Catholic mass—
and loving the music to suffering beats
and lashes from men's eyes on the Capitol streets—

Southeast DC, with its sleepy crime
my mother nursed patients from seven to nine—

patients grey from the railroad
riding past civil rights.
I walked their tracks when I entertained
them at the chapel and made their canes pillars
of percussion to my heavy gospel—
my comedy out-loud, laughing about
our shared stolen experiences of the South.

Would it surprise you if I told you my blood
was delivered from the North off Portuguese vessels
who gave me spiritual stones and the turn in my eyes—
my father's name when they conquered the Pacific Isles.
My hair is black and thick as "negrito," growing abundant
as "sampaguita" flowers—defying civilization
like Pilipino pygmies that dance in the mountain.

I could give you an epic about my way of life or my look,
and you want me to fill it in "one square box."
From what integer or shape do you count existing identities,
grant loans for the mind or crayola-white census sheets—
There's no one kind to fill for anyone.

You tell me who I am, what gets the money—
I'll sing that song like a one-man caravan.
I know arias from Naples, Tunis and Accra—
lullabyes from welfare, foodstamps and nature—

and you want me to sing one song?
I have danced jigs with Jim Crow and shuffled my hips
to the sonic guitar of Clapton and Hendrix,
waltzed with dead lovers, skipped to bamboo sticks,
balleted kabuki and mimed cathacali
arrivederccied-a-rhumba and tapped Tin Pan Alley—
And you want me to dance the Bhagvadad Gita
on a box too small for a thumbelina-thin diva?

I'll check "other." Say *artist*. That's who I am:
a poet, a writer, a lover of man.

Regie Cabico won the Grand Prize of the 1993 New York Poetry Slam and is included in the anthology *Aloud: Voices from the Nuyorican Poets Cafe* (Henry Holt, 1994). Among his television appearances are MTV's *"Free Your Mind" Spoken Word Tour*, and the PBS documentary *The United States of Poetry*. His poems appear in *IKON*, *Cocodrilo*, and *Java Journal*.

NICK CARBÓ

Little Brown Brother

I've always wanted to play the part
of that puckish pubescent Filipino boy

in those John Wayne Pacific-War movies.
Pepe, Jose, or Juanito would be smiling,

bare-chested and eager to please
for most of the steamy jungle scenes.

I'd be the one who would cross
the Japanese lines and ask for tanks,

air support, or more men. I'd miraculously
make it back to the town where John Wayne

is holding his position against the enemy
with his Thompson machine gun. As a reward,

he'd rub that big white hand on my head
and he'd promise to let me clean

his Tommy gun by the end of the night. But
then, a Betty Grable look-alike love

interest would divert him by sobbing
into his shoulder, saying how awfully scared

she is about what the "Japs" would do
to her if she were captured. In one swift

motion, John Wayne would sweep her off
her feet to calm her fears inside his private quarters.

Because of my Hollywood ability
to be anywhere, I'd be under the bed

watching the woman roll down her stockings
as my American hero unbuckles his belt.

I'd feel the bottom of the bed bounce off my chest
as small-arms fire explodes outside the walls.

I Found Orpheus Levitating

above the hood of an illegally parked red Toyota Corolla
on Mabini Street. He was tired of all that descending
into and ascending from those pretentious
New Yorker and *Atlantic Monthly* poems.
He asked me to give him new clothes so I dressed him
in an old barong tagalog and some black pants.
Because he wanted new friends in a new land, I introduced
him to Kapitan Kidlat, our local comic book hero.
But after a few whips of that lightning bolt, Orpheus
recognized Kidlat as Zeus in another clever disguise.
So, I took him to Mt. Makiling where Malakas & Maganda
(the mythical first Filipino man and woman) live
in a mansion with an Olympic-size swimming pool.
He said Maganda's aquiline features remind him
of Eurydice and Malakas has the solid torso
of a younger Apollo. He asked me to translate the word *threesome*
into Tagalog. Malakas & Maganda agreed and they stripped

Orpheus of his clothes as they led him to their giant bamboo bed.
I waited outside in the car all afternoon before he emerged
from the mansion smelling of Sampaguitas and Ylang-Ylang.
He was hungry so we drove to the nearest Kamayan restaurant
where he learned how to eat rice and pork adobo
with his bare hands. *"It's wonderful! This was the way it used to be.*
When the industrial revolution happened, all of us on Mt. Olympus
suddenly had forks and knives appear in our hands. We used
them as garden tools at first." Afterwards, he wanted to drink
and go dancing. I paid the hundred peso cover charge
for both of us at the Hobbit House in Ermita. The first
thing he did in the dark, smokey bar was trip over
one of the dwarf waiters, all the waiters were dwarfs. *"I'm sorry,*
I couldn't see. It feels as if I had just walked into a Fellini film."
He placed his hands in front of him as if he were pushing
back a glass wall. *"No, no, I'm not in a movie, I'm inside a fucking poem!*
I can see the poet's scrunched-up face on the other side
of the computer screen!" I told Orpheus to shut up or the bouncers,
                who were not
the same size as the waiters, would throw us out of the bar. We sat
in a booth across from each other and ordered us double
shots of Tanduay Rum. I asked him if he understood the concept
of "the willing suspension of disbelief." I asked him to look me straight
in the face before he ran out into the street.

The Family Tree

My grandmother had a house. My father bought it
for her after he had made his own life and
established his own family in the United States.
When I was four he sent her money to install a
wooden floor in the house. Before that she lived in
a hut. "Okay" my mother would joke, "maybe it
wasn't a *nipa* hut," but it was built on wooden
stilts. I still think of it as a tree house of sorts.

> (*nipa*
> house
> tree

> joke
> established

And that is the assignment. To build a tree with
names on it. Spanish names. Quevedo, Aguinaldo,
Ver, Edralin, Cariaga. Names from the Mysteries
of the Rosary. Concepción, Natividad, Asunción,
Encarnación. Second cousin once removed. Cross
that out. Not "Morris" like the cat on the television
commercial, but "Maurice," from "Mauricio" as in
Chevalier. It is a tree of musical notes.

> (Spanish
> cousin
> cat

> names
> removed

There are some things I should never forget. To turn the tree sideways and write down the two most important words. Noun. Verb. All you need to make a sentence is a subject and a predicate. "And from there the world is at your command." Baroque oratory, speeches, prayers, eulogies, poems. "The teachers would fine us a *centavo* each time we used an Ilocano word." But this is an American tree.

           (eulogies
           forget
           centavo

    words
    command

I shouldn't ask too many questions. Why. Why. Why. My father tells me that when I do that I am "like a monkey shakin' the tree." That's vernacular. Like 'son-of-a-gun!' It depends on how you say it. Or *'oki ni nam!'* That's very rude. More rude to say something when you don't know what you're talking about. The literal translation is gynecological. You're barking up the wrong tree.

           (monkey
           depends
           rude

    translation
    shakin'

"Black bodies swinging in the southern breeze."
My father owned a collection of old Billie Holiday records. The words were "hauntingly beautiful." He would sing a phrase, whistle a phrase, mumble a

phrase—especially when he was in a foul mood. That was the blues. I couldn't hear the song from beginning to end. It's not a ballad, but a dirge: *"Strange fruit hangin' from the poplar trees . . ."*

(mood
owned
black

bodies
whistle

It was some kind of ceremonious gesture. My father matched a tree sapling with each of his four children. Each of us took a turn at planting the sapling in a freshly dug pit of earth. Hands. Shovel. Water. My brothers were lemon and apple trees. My sister, a peach. And I, an avocado. Ripe. Fruit of our labors. After all, this is California; the bounty of each tree foretells our fate.

(hands
ripe
peach

children
turn.

CATALINA CARIAGA received her MFA in Creative Writing from San Francisco State University. She is a contributing editor for *Poetry Flash* and her poems have appeared in *ONTHEBUS* and *ZYZZYVA*.

VIRGINIA R. CERENIO

13 June 1994

my eyes wax and wane
as i hold OPEN BOAT
the book, heavy with poems
in my hands
jealous, i think
i could be here
thumbing the collection
of black-and-white photos
seeing friends, acquaintances
brothers and sisters
of color and soul
poets all
then i remember why
how she sits in my lap
already half my size
baby fingers pointing
to "dog" and "ball"
her fine waving hair
fish fins in slow waters
brushing my tired face
like the gentlest breeze
later, bottle in mouth
she will turn her head
her brown eyes searching
for my face
reaching up to touch my mouth
she will invite me to sing.

20 July 1994

my baby contemplates the toy catalog
milk bottle in mouth, pink bunny under arm
sitting on toilet, next room
i clean her dinner
enthusiastically eaten
off the carpet
disgusted at the stickiness
with each rice grain i pick up
a piece of my childhood
returns to its place in my mind
in the family album, is a picture
yellow and blue polka dots
a tent dress and party hat
the last day childhood smiled at me
kidnapped by a man with a gun

lost in rice and cleaning
        photos and memories
i listen for my baby
making filipino noises
finishing toilet
grunting with the hesitant rhythm
taught by grandmother to me
and now she's reading pictures
naming toys bears balloons

my mother

she is like this:
an ingrid bergman movie
a 1940's silver screen star
       aging gracefully
elegant, jewels tossed on like socks
wearing reeboks
she babysits in americanized pilipino top 40 radio rock-n-roll
still flirts with my 89-year-old father
girlish legs crossed
       head turned just so
always a fedora
       to match her conversation
chismis is the charm she wears in her bracelet
her worries, like dirty laundry
get whirlpool washed once a week
so unlike her sisters, in their flowered housefrocks and *tsinelas*
the rolling river behind grandfather's house
have yet to wet her delicate hands.

23 October 1992

island eyes
swallow me whole
drop like window shades
at the paleness of my husband
his lobster pink skin sunburn
his mainland english
double-checks my body language
says yes, this white man
is my husband
mine by choice
please treat him too
like mango
but the island eyes
see only the brown sister
questions swallowed with sour taste
going down
li hing mui preserved seed
suckled between tongue and teeth
sweet sour salty
salt of guilt prejudice
and a hundred years of canefields

VIRGINIA R. CERENIO's collection of poetry *Trespassing Innocence* was published by Kearny Street Workshop Press in 1989. She is a leading figure in the Filipino American and Asian American literary community. She currently resides in San Francisco where she runs her own company which provides specialized transportation services to elderly and disabled persons.

FIDELITO CORTES

Poem Composed During a Brownout

I.
This poem is being written in the dark.

It has no colors in it: no mauve,
no primrose, no periwinkle, no celadon.

It will not contain the words fast-track,
hydroelectric, coal-fired, megawatt.

In fact it will be quiet as a tomb,
like the sepulchral night on which it was born.

Later in the poem you will hear
the hum of generators.

II.
At two in the morning, in the middle
of the brownout—dreams.

Not yours, because no sleep comes to you
on this warm and windless night.

But in this unusual stillness, the city's dreams
drift up the window, gather at the foot of the bed,

look down on you and beg to be read.
So much longing and desire to shame even Freud.

Profound sex and violence. The poor dream rich dreams
and the rich dream of the simplicity of having nothing.

There is love in all the dreams.
Even the dogs dream of loving cats.

In his palace by the river, an old soldier
dreams of dragons chasing tigers.

"Unrequited love!" you sigh.
But brownouts are for lovers.

The Palace of Fine Arts in San Francisco

As though recalling a moment in Creation,
the fog lifted and everything was revealed to be

whole and beautiful, and earthly. The Palace,
losing its wisps and vapors, lost also

its nebulous celestial sheen, so that one saw
each distinct stone—solid, sepia-colored,

immutable, crannied tightly in place—
as part of this network of earth, earth, earth.

The dome squats beside the pond, a stone mammoth.
Ducks and swans swim placidly on the waters,

earthbound. The upscale houses, abutting the
Palace grounds, radiate less opulence this time

than a kind of sumtuous domestic bliss,
as at any moment the designer drapes may open

to disclose a child and parent reading together,
naming things, a luxury of certitude.

The tourists feel this in their bones, such rootedness,
a physics of objects dense and sure and solid.

Time stops at each shutter click. I, myself,
no stranger here, feel the weight of things,

and when photographed with three fellow Filipinos
just as the water sprinklers were turned on,

saw the water was quicksilver, and sensed
its cool pressure as benediction.

Fish 2

Mingling with the holiday crowd
at Union Square is like being a fish.
I tell this to my wife just now,
though it's been on my mind for a long time.
How shoppers seem to fin forward
in a kind of weird submarine logic
to the same stores we're going
and to the same bargains we want.
We jostle at toys, house wares, perfume.
Salvation Army Santas grab at our change.
Dante has a scene in the *Commedia*
describing exactly this, the converging
of fish at a ripple on the pond. A lot
of the fish look Filipino, notes my wife.

And this was what took so long to form
and to surface: that fish scatter
as easily as they converge; that many
of our fish have scattered to this place
as nannies and nurses, and store clerks
for Woolworth's and Emporium—
so many here in Union Square,
in fact, that we could claim it as ours.
Let there be jeepneys instead of cable cars!
Let there be haggling at Macy's!
Let there be *parol* and *puto bungbong!*
And let the Santas ho-ho-ho
like Filipinos, as in "Merry Christmas *ho!*
Merry Christmas *din.*" Or to go back
to the fishy, "Merry Christmas *tuyo!*"
And to you, too.

Dolce Far Niente

Sweet Saturday afternoons with nothing to do and it's spring-
        turning-into-
summer warm and wonderful. At Oliveto's there's iced tea
        and cappuccino
and a big black pot of gazpacho, and waiters entertaining some
        lounge yuppies
with talk of Arnold Schwarzenegger, Maria Shriver and Danny
        de Vito, who
dropped in Friday evening for a celebrity bite. "Arnie and
        Maria were
impatient and rude, but Mr. de Vito was a darling." Since
        Heidegger is the

only "egger" we know outside of Schwarzenegger, we skip out of
     the trattoria
with our purchase of two loaves of Italian bread and a bottle of
     olive oil,
humming "Heidegger, Schwarzenegger" to the tune of "Yes sir,
     he's my
baby." The song turns into a whistle as we catch a glimpse
     of the bay.

Then we saunter along College Avenue's mile-long strip of
     small shops and
boutiques, stopping at each window and admiring stuff we'd
     never buy even
if we had the money. The displays have all gone ethnic—blow
     pipes and bird
feathers—like most of the restaurants in the strip, which now
     serve neo-
colonial dishes from the subaltern kitchen, for the new world
     order gourmet:
Burmese, Thai, Hunan, Hunan-No MSG, Chinese Vegetarian,
     Mexican, Tex-
Mex, Cajun, Moroccan, Sicilian. We peek at the prices on the
     menus taped to
windows. Yikes! New world record prices. Time to go home.

But we're too lazy to go home. We linger at a street corner,
     not smoking.
The Italians have a name for this: sweet nothingness—that
     lingering feeling
that makes lingering feel good. Filipinos of course know this
     feeling and
know it well. Let's therefore stay here, we tell each other. Let's
     open a
Filipino dog meat restaurant for lingerers and malingerers. Let's
     call it TNT:

Food that blows up in your mouth. Let's have an open bar, a
    ferned window,
a great view, such as what we're seeing right now from this street
    corner: a
San Francisco so beautiful and unreal it seems to be floating—
    sweetly and
nothingly—on air, like Swift's Laputa. And soon to fall into the
    sea . . .
Nothing's rooted here, yet everyone wants to stay.

FIDELITO CORTES was a Wallace Stegner Fellow in poetry at Stanford
University in 1985. His first book of poetry, *Waiting for the Exterminator*
(Kalikasan Press,1989), won the Manila Critics' Circle National Book
Award in 1989. He is currently living in California with his wife, Nerissa
Balce.

SIMEON DUMDUM, JR.

Some Die of Light

Some interiors keep their shade,
Blending the floor tiles with a cool, burnt-leaf
Darkness—except perhaps one little slab
That (thanks to a chink in the roof)
Glares alone in the dusk of the interior.

Accordingly, he who finds himself inside
Will feel that the world has moved towards evening,
And rush to the door eyeing his watch,
And suddenly seeing the blazing tile
Check his foot, and lose his balance.

To My Mother

I've said good-bye many times
After that morning when with *bolos*
We were cleaning and cutting
The coconut fronds for firewood,
And I, just a boy, was your
Bungling assistant, and each time
I go away you just smile,
Remembering how, that morning,
I tired of the blade always
Flying off its wooden handle,
And thought of a trick, and decided
Not to retrieve the blade when once more

It left the knob in my hand,
And called your name, and
You screamed, seeing the handle pressed
Against my belly.

Li Pos of the Polis

Li Po drowned when he stepped into a pond
To get a piece of the moon.

Well, he was not Li Po
And it was only a puddle
And the city had many streets with pools
And many men like him
Who would rather drown themselves
In a lake of beer . . .

Besides, that moonlit night,
When he peered into that puddle,
His heart was full . . .
No, not of poetry but anger
At how the rains had dug holes in the streets,
And in his soul,

And how the holes had been untended
By time
And city hall,

And so he spat at his face in the water
Thinking it was the face of the mayor.

SIMEON DUMDUM, JR. practices law in the historically significant island of Cebu in the Philippines. He has authored two collections of poetry, *Third World Opera* and *The Gift of Sleep*. His poems are included in the anthology *This Same Sky* (Four Winds Press/Macmillan, 1992), a collection of poems from around the world, edited by Naomi Shihab Nye.

ELSA REDIVA E'DER

La Puente

(the bridge over my country)

we lived east of east L.A. / La Puente
we were latch key kids / our suburban commandments:
lock the door
don't open to strangers
make sure you turn off the stove
it's hot in L.A. / cook rice

my mother worked / making components
she built the screws that bring you the news
you'll never see her on TV / though
she speaks 4 languages:
Hawaii-pidgen
Haole
wife-speak   mother-speak

she's medicated a lot / my mom / always translating
her favorite drugs are love and jewels
we all shine
                    in her eyes

my father delivers the mail / he's a good man
but now he walks through classy neighborhoods / no one talks
to him / he fears loose dogs and people there
he's been attacked / but he's a good man

my brother Chuck / is the darkest / living in
the shadows between right and wrong / but together
we threw pinecones at passing cars

our father kicked more shit outta him than me /
told me I should know better / what does that mean
now the system that puts him on reserve / puts me
on hold / we are equal now

I have another brother / he's an acquaintance

in junior high they called me *la rascal*
we wrote a lot / our names on walls /
we all belonged / outside of walls
my best friend David—his mother still calls
him—I can hear her now—was
into glue at 11 / in juvey by 13 / in jail . . . he was a man then
I used to give him drugs from college /
I hope he's still alive

David and I and La Bridgett Fletcher
hung out growing up / for a long time
till race, class, and gender (the design of waste)
bulldozed through our street corner playground
common ground
till shame concealed our black and blues

growing up / for a long time / lost childhood
we began writing in secret
when confession, communion, confirmation
confession
taught us to lie / swallowed up our pure loyalty
growing up / for a long time / lost childhood
friends till
my parents came between their D's and my A's
Ma—the right crowd does not exist /
I look for David and La Bridgett in everyone I know.

Once We Were Farmers

Once we were farmers
and we measured time
in distant moments
of new life

and our hopes dwelled
welled up through sweat and skin
unspoken and sacred

and on the rocks we let lie in the fields
we stenciled language
and fed the rainfall upon our stories
and moments circled above the earth

      till now

      unspoken is our passion
      our passion is the moon
      lying down
      in these moments
      in the fields O pen ing
      and in the rhythms of stillness
      we were life anew

we were farmers and midwives
and blood spilled towards the future
in rituals of ancient powers

we leaned toward the cries
of children who gave sound
to rocks we let lie in the fields

We sing
we sing with eloquent hunger.

Elsa Rediva E'der was born in Hollywood and is descended from Ilocano and Visayan plantation workers in Hawaii. She is on the editorial board of *Making Waves II* and is employed at The National Asian American Telecommunications Association in San Francisco.

VIRGINIA E. ESCANDOR

Summer Nostalgia

I'd like to go home
to papaya blossoms
pinned to your hair;
to the scent of *cadena-de-amor*
from my window.
I'd like to feel
the salty air of Rizal Beach;
my sun-baked childhood—
collecting starfish
and chambered nautilus.
I'd like to see your face
once more, smiling between
bamboos with the sunset
at your back.
I'd like to sit
where a gardenia used to bloom,
listen to an old rustic harmonica,
played by a Baludian.

VIRGINIA E. ESCANDOR finished her Bachelor of Science in Nursing at Bicol University in the Philippines and she is now working at the Sloan-Kettering Cancer Center in Manhattan. Her poems have appeared in magazines in the Philippines such as *Focus, Home Life,* and *Mod.* She lives in Elmhurst, New York.

MARJORIE M. EVASCO

Dancing a Spell

Even before we begin, the sound of wind
From the old temple of *Ulun Danu* quivers
On the tips of our fingers and in our toes.
The dancer, *Ni K'tut Reneng*, knows it takes
Ten sacred years to learn one gesture
Of the wind's caress on the skin of water.

Tonight, in the shadows of our trance,
I tell my soul to grow quiet,
Become lake, reflect unbroken moon.
On the deepest part of the lake,
A solitary fisher paddles his oars.
At the shore, a woman in red sarong
Sings; their longing dances on water.

At this watershed of words,
Silence is our breath and base for music.
When the dark tones of your voice
Lay the gravel, my song will grow limbs,
Weave the oldest story, with nimble feet,
Without letting the listening ones know
We know the spellbinding name
Of the one we worship.

Elemental

In the season of this ripening,
sap of trees rise to fulfill
fruit of the topmost branch,
and the jasmine climbs the trellis
to show off a single blossom
at new moon tide.

In my garden bamboos arch
over patches of grass, river stones,
upturned earth. Alone where weeds
grow wildest, I think:

How the golden skin of mango
broke between your teeth; how
you swallowed the seamless sky
over Siquijor, your body
an entire land I could intimate
black moons from, taste of earth,
rush of river songs, smell of air
before rain, spray of flowers
with strange names. The reason

for this ripening: You are
goldened by my tongue.

Baked Oysters Rockefeller

We take shelter from the monsoon rains

In the warm inflections of dinner
Spread out to our liking, a la carte.

The sky's the old cliche: no limits here,
Chef's a master at reincarnating Lapu-lapu,
Or carving a plateful of Manansala's heart.

Will I, I wonder, be so bold as to say
With a straight face to the waiter: we are
Carnal, you see, hungry for the Other.

And we'd like everything as raw as we
Can get it in this civil place, with its piano,
Violin, china, silver, spotless linen.

You look at me, intent, your voice encodes
Bite-sized pleasures—(*Kani Sushi,* Yes?),
Dipped desires—(*Oysters Rockefeller,* baked?).

My mind scuttles the crab's tangent
To our table, unshelled; my tongue
Sauces at the thought of succulents.

Even when the waiter interjects
Those Rockefellers are out of season,
He'll never guess what the feast's absence meant.

Heron-Woman

This gift of story
From your mother's old country

Tells the songs behind my ears
To unfurl white wings
Of the Great Heron.

Water has the texture of memory:
Once, a child listened to her father
Call the herons from the green paddies.

In the silence of attention,
I am Heron-Woman,
Weaving feathers into silk,
Shimmering like the waters
Of a blue estuary.

At twilight I glide to shore,
Fold my body into
The sheath of solitude.
Slender in vigil,
I dream of light
Catch the quick
Flash of silver
In water.

And I
Am still
Once
More.

MARJORIE M. EVASCO is the author of *Dream Weavers: Selected Poems 1976-1986*. She has received residency fellowships to Bellagio, Italy and Hawthornden Castle, Scotland, and is currently Associate Director for Poetry at De La Salle University in Manila.

Balitaw

Maybe the winds die down tomorrow,
Maybe the heavens be quiet, settle down.
Friday the 13th—two trains collide, it says in the papers
While the wind howls. Give it up! Love it when the wind blows.
She holds her black skirt down against her legs
Laced in black, in the middle of the morning.
Dreams reverberate beneath the ground of my feet
Shake me up & I say to myself—
Go get a job, get your shit together.
Dreamt of having an affair with Marilyn Monroe
Before she became famous. Playfully cupped
Her big wonderful breasts with a plunger.

Only in dreams can one do this, Thank God.
Eight Pilipinos crucified themselves this year.

Kundiman

she retires from life's uncertainties, he plunges
into its rivers, lingers in tributaries
she remembers the time of day, the quality of light
he drowns in dark rivers of lethe

she knows herself through the minds of others
he hides within shrines of imaginings
she thrives on a touch of affection
he cringes at the thought & flees from a kiss

she goes to gallavant in forests north
he wanders in deserts south
she wakes when first light rises east
he, when sun sinks mountains west

she, the bird of winged flight, he, the mole
she wakes—a caliper, he in dreams—a rose

BATAAN FAIGAO is a highly respected master of Ta'i Chi which he teaches at The Naropa Institute in Boulder, Colorado. He has published two collections of poetry, *Infinite Longings* (1969) and *In Celebration of Strange Gods* (1984). Among his awards are literary grants from the Boulder Arts Council in 1982 and 1984.

LUIS H. FRANCIA

The Secret in the Roar

I.
We were gestures of the ocean once
Which we, having no need to

Understand, understood.
By coral, by sun

Were we blessed, and in those currents
That were our bone and sinew, we were

More than our thoughts
Could utter. Though we had no

Compass for existence
The rough charge

Of being ran deeper than
Fear.

Before pterodactyl and tiger
Grew, before the heave of rock

From water, before the first walk
Before memory

Were we elemental, were we
This very globe.

II.
Ages thence, myself a wanderer on the
Shore flings himself into the waves

Out of desire
Out of deep discontent

A query long hurled and
Hurling at the sea.

What matter, matrix?
Matters.

Flings himself, now of upright
And sun-baked flesh, listening for

The roar's secret, the
Surf's knowing voice.

The waters tug as at a
Familiar (a reply he senses,

Blood echoing) daily
Remembered in orisons ceaseless

Upon the shore, that altar
Of pebble and sand.

He thinks and sings the sea
As the sea sings him, its

Arms of waves half-raised in
Remembered loss, half in unheralded

Joy, there moving in the light

A poet ambivalent in his griefs

Of love, mourning, shouting
The lyrical ancestral poem.

Video Victim

I am Moses awaiting
Apotheosis. I am mighty
Ape, with Fay! in his heart.
I am Edward the God of
Crazy. I am Fearless Frank,
Slayer of chickens.
My solitude is stereo
Simulcast throughout the
Unpromised land. I am a ball,
A bag, a beer bottle, Mamon
Arising from dish rags.

I should have been a pair of jeans
Scuttling across corporate floors.

Through realms of drain-pipe
I travel, I sing of combustion
Chambers, the well-scrubbed
Priest of gastro-intestinal
Salvation. Madagascar and Paris,
Guadalupe and Cartagena call
While I sail in a Sea of Pure
Fizz by the shores of Plop-plop.
Soda rivers unite with sky

While running noses run dry.
I am everywhere and nowhere,

Everyone and no one.
I am Veni, Video, Victim.

I, Imperator, demand a Liberator.

In Gurgle Veritas

I gurgled straight out of my
   Mother's womb
I gurgled at the gargoyle of a world that
   Leered at me
I bit my mother's breast and gurgled
   Her milk and blood
I gurgled through childhood and
   Adolescence
I gurgled at the sprouting of my sex
I gurgled when my parents made love
   And stabbed each other
I gurgled at noon, I gurgled
   When the wolves howled at the moon
I gurgled when they raised the flag
   And asked me to pledge allegiance
I gurgled at the ballot box
I gurgled when Mahatma, Martin, Malcolm and
   Ninoy went down
I gurgled at the insolence of heaven
   That would not keep
Our innocence

I gurgle at the death of Earth
    And the indifference of the stars

And when the Big Boys came with
    Their guns intent on murder
Still I gurgled. I gurgled when
My arms were cut off
    When they lopped off my
Feet I gurgled still
They fed me my balls and stuffed
My brains in my ass
    Still I gurgled
This incomparable mantra
This vast vegetable of incomprehensibility
    Taking root even
In death
Yes I gurgle them all
Priests and politicians,
    Matrons and Messiahs, purveyors of
Rot, dust and treacherous love
I'll gurgle them
    Through the years and spin
    Them in my mouth and spit them
Out like a tale with a bitter ending
Raise the banners
    Of your reason, Jack, and feast on
Your white gods, I'll
Raise my dark lyrics, and toast and
Roast you with my sweet kiss, and the
    Lucifer lunacy of gurgle.

is there There in dying

is there There
        in dying (leaving

the paleness of what
        are) an Always to rejoice

Godlike, and that
        a voice, when empty of

change for its
        muse, for government

of tongue, the rhyme
        the range be winged by

a scheme of light?
        and yet forever flows

the sea of creation.
        nor poets nor Poetry

sulk: living is the
        lock, dying is the key.

Luis H. Francia has won a Palanca Memorial Award in poetry and is the editor of *Brown River, White Ocean: An Anthology of Twentieth-Century Philippine Literature in English* (Rutgers University Press, 1993) and the author of the collection of poetry *The Arctic Archipelago and Other Poems* (Ateneo de Manila University Press, 1991). He is based in New York City where he is a contributing editor for *The Village Voice*.

ERIC FRUCTUOSO

Astig

there u guys go
standing on that corner
drinkin' the 40 dogs and
gettin' all tweaked on *damo*
while the fat beets are bumpin'
out of junior's car
"yeeeaah and you don't stop
'coz it's a 1-8-7 on an undercover cop"
that song is the bomb kid!
a car rolls by and everyone tenses up
they check to see if it's anybody they know
rollin' in that dropped honda civic
just stand the passengers down
you never know, right
it might be those muhfuckers
who rolled up on us last week at serramonte
i'm ready to take them mark-ass busters out
one of the boys walk up
"FUCK all that gangbangin' shit,
I ain't even into that
knowhutamsayin'?"
I just wonder how true his statement is
considering his current state of boodahfied funk
one of the fellas is so drunk,
he pisses in the middle of the street
not giving a fuck about lola
peeking out her window checking
to see if anything is being vandalized
3 more carloads roll up
more homies coming to chill in tha hood

everyone's eyes are shot to the redness
smokin' dat muhfuckin' chronic
that's tha shit homee
blunts, that's an east coast thang
we is strictly west coast chronic smokin' muhfucks!
thass tha reel deal!
lola takes another peek out her window
spyin' on tha guys that she once remembered
as nice little boys who went to the catholic school
around the corner
somebody yells up at her
"lola, baka gusto niyong damo?"
everyone bursts out in chaotic laughter
drunk out of their skulls and high as fuck
as lola nervously hides behind her curtain
another car rolls up and
everyone's trippin'
"pare, it's a red prelude,
mukhang lima sila."
the adrenaline is pumpin'
their trigger fingers are itchy

the car slowly creeps and everybody
just dogs the shit out of the passengers,
a chinese family, lookin'
scared out of their skulls
"hindi sila pare," somebody yells
i just wonder what would've happened
if it was . . .

ERIC FRUCTUOSO works as a delinquency prevention counselor in
San Francisco.

ERIC GAMALINDA

Denials

Not this room.

      Not the rain drumming
small figures on the roof.

Not this shadow play
across the window

this python bridge
shirking into estuary

and motel, mosque
and citadel.

      Rivers
on whose banks the most destitute
of peoples wake to a year
of eclipses.

Not the neon from whose light
the icons of Quiapo borrow their miracles.

Not these streets.

Not the smoke rising like stallions from
          sewers,

nor the river with its torques and silverfish.

And certainly not this room.

                    Again I say
there will be some residue
that can no longer attempt a memory.

Not this city that taught you its hatred.

Not these nights on smokey streets
and the women lonely
and unbelieving

not the lights on the bay
not this scapular of automobile lights.

Always a note beyond the scale,
a color beyond all shades;

not the music and the silences,
not these violent sunsets
caught, like a rainbow still pulsing,
in the grey nets of electrical wires.

Lament Beginning w/a Line after Cavafy

Manila is full of the black ruins of my life.
The beggars beg for mercy and the children die
in war or peace. It has spoken nothing to me
these thirty years. I have found in it
neither love nor solitude; I spoke to it in vernaculars
of its sex, in a language it should understand
but always fails to. Everything I lose
converges there. The women, tungsten-raw, sitting by the windowsills.

Young boys shimmering like eels. And always among them
the shadows I divulge: black holes and black spaces.

La Naval De Manila:
Selim Sot as a Modern Political Observer

Things turn mortal at twilight.
Six years at sea, and I am attuned
to the skulls of mystery: that dark
should spare no one, arrabal

of moonlight is love's betrayal.
I say I am unmoved by it.
I have met the opportune fevers
where they dawdle or malinger.

Staggering into the *avenidas*
de las felicidades I burn
where it matters: I claim dominion
over oracles, wounds. All this mourning

distends the senses, plucks from star
or sprint of cloud some vast
insouciant theophany, wanton
hope in the province of gods, et

cetera. I have seen night's dogs
howl and scratch the tombstones
for my name. I have watched the hands
move where they may, contraband

but beautiful in the dusklight
with hint of down and Faure hissing,
melancholy on the tape. I have said
the proper words, bled just so, disbursed

such promises as vow eternity; in short
I've made my peace. And the little that I vow
I disenthrall so often. My words, sure and fluid
as meteors, assume the orbits

of beatitudes, bright testaments.
What am I then, sputtering syllabi
of supernovas? Another dragon?
I scuttle to the naked christ

who skims along the muscled seraphim
and is moved by instinct to extinguish me.
Now all the world stoops to accept
his benediction, while forgotten armies

sludge across the sleepy cenacles
where admirals exhume their favored
speech, figments of their $x\,y\,z$'s.

Light Falls Obliquely:

For Celine

And what more do we know of it,
and the world slanted by its shifty haze?
That it bends in the soft ecliptic
and there moves with the weight of its passing,

or is so moved: and we are its burden
of what? memory and denials,
everything we leave
for the little that we bear of it:
this slow, deliberate reprieve.
I still say we can't know more of our lives
but the minutest spectrum
we allow our faintest hopes,
and therein survive.

If light falls obliquely,
does the world follow accordingly,
the way leaves trace the spirals
of wind as they fall
magnificent as storms to their death?
We know this much: that in death
no wind nor angels mourn
and so the earth persists
as its own final sacrifice, all
intimations of amber. If we leave it at that,
will the light pick it up,
toss its umbrage to view?

Will memory cease to be memory
in another light?

We ask and earth's silence
makes these distances sadder than they ought to be.
We know enough of the planet, yes,
but little of its strength and implications;
in short, the little that matters.
Look at it this way: history
seems less bizarre in time,
no more than epic eccentricities;
all love dissolves to romance; we are forgiven

all of the above.

We look askance, approaching drift
and descent with little reflection.
Some people would call this enlightenment.

ERIC GAMALINDA has received residency fellowships from Bellagio, Italy; Hawthornden Castle, Scotland; The Corporation of Yaddo; and The McDowell Colony in the U.S. He is one of the Philippine's foremost and innovative novelists as well as an accomplished poet. His most recent collection of poetry is *Lyrics from a Dead Language* (Anvil, 1991). He lives in New York City.

EDWARD CORTEZ GARRETT

Grandfather's Mint

Because he loved his rooster, and his wife
grew jealous-ill, mornings he would rise
   from his chosen sofa—
put on a white shirt and leather slippers,
chinelas, and descend to the coop

to smoke his brown *tabacalera.* And he would
blow circles about the ruby, sapphire, and gold
   plumage of the bird
while pointing to the sun above the thatch,
the banana tree's jade fronds.

Jump, he'd show it, and hang in midair.
Fall but turn and kick, he'd say. Slash
   with the blade. All it takes
to sail from this sick place.
And yet, upstairs his wife would call him

back to room and bed where he would stand
with medicine and spoon—pulled, pulling
   from his wife and her
unbearable grasp. He gasped to be free
of *better or worse,* the promise that he gave

and would prefer to forget. Her eyes, larger
than the sea with its mountains, seemed to say
   I am all the distance you will need.
But all he saw was the fisherman's outrigger, sails
like a flag, ready for wind, the real stuff of cockpits.

The Bachelors

The message, we conclude, is inevitable—
standing before the bird-of-paradise—
leaves, twin plumed fire hovering as wings,
      mimicking the hummingbird as it goes
         downward with its beak,
probing past a grey petal to nectar,
wet elixir of sun and rain.

Romance between foreigners! And what intelligence
to believe in the plant's obvious pretense!
We look at the sky, giddy with wind
      and those forbbiden things—the women,
         like rain iridescent, gowned
in unmistakable bloom, the ribald aroma
that speeds a wanderer home.

We laugh, and still laughing depart for the table
where a punchbowl of rose brims, offering
a ladle into the chill of voluptuous ice—
      all around the sugared enticements
         of bread and fruit, whatever brings
a man from delicious alone forward to vermillion,
cheeks flushed with rouge, eyelids and orgasm of blue.

EDWARD CORTEZ GARRETT received an MA in Creative Writing from the University of Florida, Gainesville. He is currently teaching Speech and English Literature at the Laredo Community College in Laredo, Texas.

JEAN V. GIER

Going Baroque

*In order that this fortress have walls capable of resisting
attacks by the Europeans, he orders that the cement be mixed
with the blood of hundreds of bulls. That is marvelous.*
"The Baroque and the Marvelous Real"
Alejo Carpentier

Bad Taste
is one place to begin, where
the impulse to ornament is a cast off
from the columnar ruins; add to this an excess
of emotion, a lyric feeling
a swelling of the humours and of the rib
cage as the histamine pours forth, filling
the cavities of the lungs;
at times the heart
and even the eyes bleed, a stigmata
in reaction to strangeness, to creatures half
horse, half man, the Bethlehem
Beast: *lo real maravilloso.* Yes, the will
to elaborate continues on its own:
bodily fluids seep like the tears
of polychromed saints
red and ochre out of cartoon
gargantuans, giant malls, flea markets,
mga tikbalang; graffiti and saucer-eyed
cats and chihuahuas
outstrip the dainty bodies
of rococo angels and putti.

In the midst of this, you pull out a dictionary,
the *Pequeño Larousse*, no less;
in your hands I see a tiny book bound in red
velvet and gilt, the words spilling
over the the edges like so much
Halloween candy. So hard to choose:
Churrigueresque is a good word, and *criollo;*
barroquismo for its extravagance,
its lust for movement, for the violated
grottos and bas-reliefs
of the East.

Or is it the West?
It depends on which direction
you are sailing, at which port you wish to be
anchored, on what thorny rose you pull out
of your chest. Shall we pretend
that Classicism is
not a verb for power;
that the stench rising
from a hundred slaughtered bulls
is as fragrant as a passage from Proust?
It all depends on the accumulation
of capital, the ability to cover distance,
the desire to mold and sculpt the human cry until
it becomes a perfect example of the *Magic
Flute* or the embroidered strawberry
hankie of *Othello,* until
the temple at Mitla becomes Diabelli's theme
by Beethoven, until the very flesh
gives way to spontaneous
growths that stand up and buttress the secret
dictator in you, the labyrinthine cathedral
in your backyard with its abraded
stone gargoyles that (have you noticed?)

gaze down on you as if
you were full of sin, full
to bursting
they piss on you in the rain.

And yet, bad taste
is a place to begin.
Where the impulse
to ornament casts off
from the columnar
ruins.

*"We have, on the other hand, the baroque, a constant of the human
spirit that is characterized by a horror of the vacuum, the naked
surface, the harmony of linear geometry, a style where the central
axis . . . is surrounded by reproductions of what one might call
proliferating nuclei . . ."*

"The Baroque and the Marvelous Real"
Alejo Carpentier

Examining the I

1. Say the words I am.
tease out the meaning and
here among the pressing many
interrogate identity. Talking
talking always to perfect;
each one a fluctuation a
movement to close to
open to draw out.

II. The words. Write them
again and again a baroque
entablature the facade of
a cathedral. A *plenaria,*
the professor says, elaborating
on the extension of emotion.
Wriggling in a petrie dish. Look
at that: a colony, the whole
thing emoting, cilia, many
moving across glass across
the slide stained red with dye.

III. We were examining a character
in a novel. If I look I am
the one, and I am also. The eye.
Anger that comes over and over
a bright difficulty a fracture
of the different coming into
a focus like pain. But the thing
itself is not that. Colonizing
oneself the little fusions
building, exploding, split apart.

IV. To place it where
it can be viewed from
a distance. Held to this
proximity and seeing it also
from outside the edifice.

The experience of fear of *lightning*
a deep internal shock crossing
the night sky. The sound of its
arrival travels through
my body.

California Coast

The Ohlone walk among us, setting fire to the stipa;
their fields of vast burning among the freeways

and condominiums deposit ash upon the sand
upon the decaying shells of white sand clam,

the many littleneck clams. *Holy Mary, mother of God
the Lord is with thee,* the catechumens chant

as they march around the mission chapel. Father Serra
proselytizes among the clapper rails, the furious

scrub Jays, as seams open in the sidewalks and visionaries
come forth, singing of fishes and loaves, planets aligned,

Rahjneesh, Eckankar (we will consume anything: snakes,
God). The Pomo still eat the chiton, chew the tough

flesh, discarding the sandy carapace. It is said
Jaime de Angulo plowed his ledge of land 2000 ft.

above Torre Canyon in his all-together. Died sad
and crazy, having lost his European manners

and his son to the rubbled cliffs. I know
there is a rocky ledge beyond which all things

fall away; the ground shudders beneath our beds
and we prick up like frightened ground squirrels

hearing a sound like the Southern Pacific about to derail
in the front yard. Now and then, one of us plunges

into the starry field of excess and awe.

A First View of the Islands

I.
Five miles beneath the fuselage I see
Green, or deeper: a cartographer's
teal blue—that color staining
the canyons and drowned

precipices of the Moro Gulf on a map.
But this is rainforest: trees, giant ferns
tiered and canopied

up the hillsides, the earth seeming
so fecund it disappears
under tendrilous and leafy offspring.

Like the Monkey-eating Eagle, we
travelers are all shadow, raptor
over the Cordillera, intent on a dream.
Below, dung beetles

collect their stoppers of earth, fire ants
string themselves like rosary beads
across rivulets. The saints, too,

flourish in this latitude: Our Lady
of the Pillars, the Santo Niño in his
stiff, red velvet and gold stitching;

II.
even so, the *diwata* creaks in the *narra*
trees, demands recompense.

III.
Zamboanga del Norte, Samar, Leyte Gulf.
Mist closes over heights and depths,
no in-between. But ninety kilometers north

it's all grey plain, a bank of stratocumulus
wants to rain ashes on the city below
and does:

two righteous fingers of concrete
poke up through the wool and pour smoke
which settles and settles, pressed down

by the heaviness of a thousand stations
of heaven; pantheon of the *Bontoc, Ifugao,
Kalinga* . . . Christ takes his place among them.

We tighten the cords on our belongings.
I feel the tilt of the turn as we
descend. Across the aisle,

one fat child vomits before the doors
open in the belly of the plane and
the wheels lock down into place—
        before the painted dream becomes
        something else.

JEAN V. GIER is a second generation Filipina born in San Francisco and raised in Santa Cruz, California. Her poems appear in *Poetry Flash, Proliferation,* and *Berkeley Poets Cooperative.* She is a PhD candidate in English at the University of California, Berkeley.

EUGENE GLORIA

Assimilation

On board the Victory Line Bus
boring down Kennon Road
from a weekend in Baguio
is the bus driver's sideline:
a Coleman chest full of cold Cokes and Sprites,
a loaf sack of sandwiches
wrapped in pink napkin and cellophane.
My hunger sated by thin white
bread thick with mayonnaise,
diced pickles and slim slice of ham.
What's mere snack
for my gaunt Filipino seatmate,
was my American lunch, a habit
of eating, shaped by boyhood shame.
You see, there was a time when I believed
that a meal meant at least a plate of rice
with a sauced dish like *kare kare,*
or *pinakbet* pungent with *bagoong.*
But homeboys like us are marked
by experience of not being part of the whole
in a playground full of white kids lined
on red-painted benches in the fall chill of noon,
lunchpails bright with their favorite cartoons,
and a thermos of milk, or brown paper sacks
with Glad bags of chips, peeled Sunkist,
Mom's special sandwich with crisp leaf of lettuce,
and pressed turkey thick in between—
crumbed with the breakfast table bread.

I remember that first day of school, my motherwith the purest intention,
took two sheets of foil hollowed
with a cup of steamed rice
and a helping of last night's
caldereta: chunks of potatoes, sliced
red peppers, and a redder sauce with beef;
and I, with hunger, could not
bring myself to eat.
Ashamed to be more different
than what my face had already betrayed,
the rice, I hid from my schoolmates.
Next morning, my mother grasped
the appropriate combination: fruit,
sandwich cut in two triangles,
handful of chips, my best broken English.
And weeks passed while the scattered rice—
beneath the length of that red-painted bench—
blackened with the schoolyard's dirt.

Touch

What this driver knew of touch
I had to relearn an ocean away.
Sampaloc unfolding before us
as I stared with mouth ajar
at Manila's decaying buildings,
dour rain-soaked wood, colonial:
Spanish, or American,
it hardly mattered.

And yet the streets teemed with life
as my driver went on with the politics
of touch, a common man's perception
concerning what is lacking and what
is gained from a culture that weans girls
to walk hand-in-hand and boys arm-in-arm,
as common as daylight on the streets
that it is touch, he'd say,
that makes us a people.

I will not sentimentalize
this driver's innocent wisdom.
What he knows is simply
what is given him as I take this knowledge
in remembering how often my lover
wanted to hold my hand
when we walked outside,
how much I disliked
such affection because I felt possessed.
And a poorer reason, because I feared affection.
Maybe in this nation of the flesh,
distance will hold us together,

as I try to remember her bent low
to the bleeding heart's small petals,
and around us, buds of wild lilies
where once there was a shallow gorge
that dipped into the clearing and horses
claimed the fields; and that one night
she couldn't sleep, she walked

into that same field to behold
the stars she once named for me.
Maybe now I will understand what secrets
she wanted to share that night

while I pretended to sleep.
Years later, we returned to that place
only to discover that the rains
have flooded the field into a lake,
as if all memory was fiction,
as if memory had turned things around.
Drowned in Manila traffic, the driver
maneuvered our car into an open lane
where in a sea of cars
not one touches the other.

Aleng Maria

Silent as a nun Aleng Maria prays,
her false teeth float in a half-filled glass
beside the votive candle, the only light
for her Santo Niño. In this sleeping hour,
the woman we've called a bag-of-hard-howls
is mumbling her words as we unfurl our mats.

Mosquito nets sag over our sleep mats
as our landlord below prays
with eyes as wide as an owl's.
Her false teeth drink from a glass
beside her red votive cup. This is the hour
she finds solace within a candle's light.

Aleng Maria glows within the light
of her votive candle, her rolled-up straw mat
leans like a bamboo cane for another hour
while she continues to pray

for her children—now ghosts, transparent as glass.
When the moon is full we can hear them howl.

The prodigal moon makes all creatures howl—
like Aleng Maria who chases us when she's all lit
up from the tuba she drinks from a glass—
unless she dips straight from a vat
which poor Aleng Maria prays
would never dry up. If that hour

ever comes, oh, that awful hour
when her ghost children prowl
her house and she's too drunk to pray,
I would be the first to light
a candle for Santo Niño, pray that her vat
would fill up—just enough for a glass.

Aleng Maria grabs the half-filled glass
where her teeth soaked for several hours.
And like a cigar, rolls her brightly colored mat
as she begins another day with a chilling howl
"Goddam kids, get da fuck outta my sight!"
Her curses, solemn as prayer.

I bless that bag-of-hard-howls who lights
a candle beside a glass and prays. In this hour,
we listen for ghosts on our sleep mats.

Rizal's Ghost

Once on a train from Baden-Baden,
fields beneath gray skies

looked like loneliness that made you strong.
A staccato of steel against grinding steel,

each lurch, each shove of that swift machine,
became one thought and then another,

an intaglio of memory pressed
against a sheet of layered landscapes:

that first sunrise burning through a net
of tule fog in the Sacramento Delta;

that once I slept on damp night grass
and drowned beneath an ocean of stars;

that moonset beyond the curve of bay.
I'd cut my hand in Baden-Baden,

sucked blood from the same hand
in Nice: the bread, the brie,

the cold slice of salami salted
from my blood-stained knife.

I recalled the flowers from Hiedelberg,
fragrantless and flat between

Jose Rizal's journal; the petal's cup,
violet and white, so kind to his eyes.

Once in the Black Forest I unfolded
my handkerchief in which I had taken

dark bread from my hostel's table.
As I moistened it with rain,

Jose Rizal's ghost crossed
my wooded path, a purple flower

in one hand, a clean bullet hole
through his breast. A broken whisper

breathed from his ashen lips.
"Never forget this flower,"

he began in sotto voce, "Never forget
the sky which saw its birth."

I clasped the flower from his hand,
the moistened bread I left in his.

I passed two hikers on my way,
their voices thick as the knapsacks

they carried. They were Americans,
their language for a moment unlike my own.

Eugene Gloria recently spent a year and a half in Manila as a Fulbright Exchange Scholar after having received an MFA in Creative Writing from the University of Oregon. His poems have appeared in *Mid-American Review, Parnassus, Quarry West*, and in the anthology *The Open Boat* (Anchor Books, 1993).

N.V.M. GONZALEZ

A Wanderer in the Night of the World

She made him an amulet
Of two slices of ginger,
And three cloves of garlic,
And then said: Go, for soon enough
It will be dark. . . .

The bulge grew
Upon the skin of his shirt,
A light sac over his heart.

He stubbed his toes on a rock
While crossing the yard.
      Sorry, *Ginoong* Rock,
      But I must be on my way.

From the river he headed
To a waiting banca.
He got himself across, singing
      Goodbye, *Ginang* River.
      And be around, *Manang* Banca,
      When I return . . .

Then Nature called
Before Banca could answer,
Before River could say
      Keep well
      And remember . . .

So it had to be:
By the nearest tree he stopped

Although not without saying,
      Let me be disrespectful, *Mamang* Tree.
      As I must travel light.

      In the night of the world
      Journeys can be long, said Tree.
      In the night of the world,
      Totoong totoo,
      So it is told.

He found his way.

The Deepest Well in Madras

Here, she said, is your deepest well in Madras.
Drop a pebble if you like
This very minute,
And only by morning
Will you hear the splash below—
Only after your dream
Of haunted bridges,
Wooden railings askew,
Bicycles without riders—
Only then will you catch
The quintessential echo.

Hungry stones gird this wall;
A sturdy breed,
They breakfast on anguish,
Skip lunch and, finally,
Dine on despair.

In the sunlit yard
Nine blind children watch,
Their mouths agape,
Flyblown-dry, in wonder.

How the Heart Aches

The people who live here
Have been at each other's throats,
Yelling and stumping about,
Banging doors, knocking furniture down.
But now, in exhaustion, one has retreated to a corner;
Another paces about, sniffling;
A third has turned to mending her blouse.
A fourth, drawing the dusty blinds,
Has yielded to a fit of sneezing.
Salute! says the fifth one, braiding her hair.

They are a lovely family
Although quarrels are essential to their style.
The peace around here, on some evenings,
Could come round like the moon,
The air laced with the smell of spareribs
Over hickory embers.

But who's this one
Who has made it to the door, valise in hand,
A tote bag over his shoulder?
He isn't even turning around
To bid you good-bye.

I Made Myself a Path

I made myself a path on the side of a hill
This summer in Halifax.

> You'll meet some of your countrymen there,
> Priscilla had written, putting away her notes
>   on Ibo folklore.

To pluck me from the airport,
Bob Adams, tall and Jamaican, was on hand
With his son, Peter, curly-haired,
A high school kid bound for Science—
Such is the confidence of the young.

> Driving into Dartmouth,
Thence into Halifax town,
Past the cemetery where survivors of the *Titanic*
Lay buried. . . . It struck me then, and this I told Bob,
How that very moment I had come full circle.
>   Once, in knee-pants,
>   I asseverated *This is the forest primeval*
>   Ruler-straight out of Longfellow,
>   Knowing then only hexameters and nothing else whatsoever
About the Evangeline that he himself did not see.

How correct Priscilla was: discoverers of a kind
My compatriots have become nurses and doctors
In alien shores. They've ventured forth
And gotten lost here in Halifax,
In forests of cedar and aspen
Stunned by salt-sodden rock
Crushed by quiet waters that once bore a prince on a visit
To his princess at a lodge on an island shore.

He built her the lodge, as John put it. It was John
In whose veins ran Knox and Howie blood.
Now he drove his old Dodge
Into Wolfville, tracing his ancestry
As far back as the mid-eleven hundreds in Scotland,

Bridges we crossed and white road markers for speedsters
We passed. Yes, yes, he said. Now, what of yours?
No farther than Evangeline's?

In the afternoon sun, later,
The better for us to admire
Both the melancholy and happy sides of her face
(Because the sculptors, a father-and-son team,
Worked it out thus, you might know, said Robert McDonald,
Adding, "Not plaid but tartan, please!")

We joined other pilgrims
That Continental Trailways chaperoned
Dutifully in the summer twilight hour.

Such as Arcadie, Grand Pre;
Or how a page of childhood turned to life.
For a breather, a real sub rode
The water off Princess Lodge—of all places.
After three months of 20th century Atlantic weather.
Which Prince was visiting this time around?

I discovered, thus, my side of the hill
Strewn with flowering shrubs
That had no names
But did not call me a stranger.

Emboldened, the grass knowing my every step,
On occasion a gouty limp,

I made myself that path
Along the slope, and wore it firm
With a week's lordship—incorrigible of me,
Awake to all this living,
This wonder.

N.V.M. Gᴏɴᴢᴀʟᴇᴢ was born in 1915 in Romblon, Romblon. He was only nineteen years old when four of his early poems were published by Harriet Monroe in the January, 1934 issue of *Poetry: A Magazine of Verse*. One of the Philippine's most distinguished writers, he is Emeritus Professor of English at California State University, Hayward, and has authored three novels and five collections of short stories, the most recent being *The Bread of Salt and Other Stories* (University of Washington Press, 1993).

VINCE GOTERA

Manong Chito Tells Manong Ben about His Dream over Breakfast at the Manilatown Cafe

Ah, good morning, 'Pare. *Kumusta naman?*
Have you eaten yet? Hoy, Johnny!
Bring my friend Ben some coffee, OK?
Putang ina! The service in here gets worse
every day, ha? *Ayan,* here he comes.

You know, Ben, when you walked in the door,
this dream I had last night just jump—like that—
into my head. I was back home, a kid
again, maybe fifteen or sixteen, two years
before I come here. I was with this girl—
I didn't see her for forty-five years
until last night. I ever tell you about her?
'Pare, we was supposed to get married
but then I come stateside and that—goddamn—
was the end of it. I don't know . . . the letters
stopped and I just got too busy with blondies.
You know how it was, Ben. Those blondies.

Anyway, Maria Clara—yeah, that
was her name, no kidding—Maria Clara and I
were down by the river. Saturday morning, I think,
she wasn't the kind to play hooky, you know?
What's that? Chaperone? I remember wondering
about that, too, in my dream. Her papa
used to send her little brother Pabling
all over with us—what a pain in the ass
that little kid was. But, no, not this time.
Just Maria Clara and me. Now listen,

Ben, what I'm gonna tell you now
happen only in my dream, OK?
It's not a real memory, nothing like that.

Maria Clara was teasing me, asking
if I could swim, and I say, sure I could.
And she say, well prove it, there's the water.
And so I take off my shirt and then my pants . . .
I hesitate a second, look around,
and pull off my underwear too. She puts
her hand on my shoulder, and I turn to look at her.
Our eyes meet—*ay naku,* Ben,
she got beautiful eyes, real dark,
like when you look into a well at night
and see stars down there. You know that painting
by Juan Luna, the really famous one
in Malacañang Palace, *La Bulaqueña?*
Maria Clara was beautiful like that.
Anyway, she looks in my eyes, she never looks down,
and then she reaches over and holds my *titi.*
I was getting hard by then, anyway.
It was like it really happened, *'Pare.*
I can still feel her hand, her fingers
were cold, I feel each one as she closes her hand.
Then I turn back to the water and I dive in.

That woke me up. I'm sitting there, sweating
and cold. Jesus, I left the window open,
you know, so I get up, close the window,
walk down the hall to the bathroom, and piss
it all away. It all just goes away.
I forget all about that dream until
I see you walk in here. *Susmariosep,*
that's the problem with you and me, Ben.
That's the problem with all of us Pinoys.

116

We piss it all away. We come here thinking
America—yeah, gold grows on the trees
like mangoes—and it breaks our hearts, 'Pare.
Yeah, that's it—we piss it all away.
Here, have another cup, Ben.
Hoy, Johnny! Bring us more coffee, OK?
Putang ina, the service here is terrible.

Madarika

—*Since the 20s, the International Hotel, on the edge of San
Francisco's Chinatown, had housed the manongs—the pioneer
Filipino immigrants to America. In 1977, young Filipino
Americans fought the eviction of these "old-timers" and the
demolition of the "I-Hotel" by linking arms against the wreck-
ing ball—for many of them, the event was an emblem of their
awakening into Filipino American history and culture.*

—Madarika, *in Tagalog, means "homeless wanderer."*

You ask me my name? They got lotsa names
for me—Frankie, Manong Chito, Old-Timer—
you walk into a Chinese restaurant with me,
you see they call me "Amigo." Lotsa names.
But I'm just a Pinoy, you know? *Pinoy,*
that's a password. You see a stranger across
the street, his hair shiny with Brilliantine,
just like a rooster's dark-blue feathers after
the owner spits down the neck and head at a cockfight.
So you yell out, "Hey, Pinoy?" If the answer

come back, *"Hoy, Kababayan,"* then you know that stranger's
a friend: he'll stand at your back in a knife fight.

Anyway, my name is Francisco X. Velarde.
X for Xavier. So you see I got a powerful
patron saint. I was born in Ilocos Norte
in 1906. I still remember the sunrise
back home. I was the youngest of seven boys
and it was my job to take our *kalabaw*
to the field in the morning. I remember lying
on his broad back, gray like an elephant. The sun
climbing between his horns as he walked, first
the pink spreading across the sky like flowers.

Only another place I see something
like that was Alaska where I ended up
at a cannery in '24. It never got dark,
you know, but when the sun would sink below
the horizon, the sky would light up in purple
and pink just before sunrise. All day we slave
on the line. My job is cutting off fish heads.
One time, my *kumpadre* Paulino cuts his finger
right off but we never find it. You young Pinoys,
you never know how hard we worked at that cannery,
and it was dangerous, too. But every night
we were our own boss, and we played baseball—
fast-pitch, slow-pitch—in the midnight sun.

I worked lotsa jobs. Barber, farm
worker, dishwasher, houseboy, janitor: you name it,
I done it. Every place I been—in Alaska,
in Seattle, in Stockton cutting asparagus—
they got these dance halls. A dime for a dance.
These days, a dime don't seem like much to you,
but you know it was a lot in the 30s.

118

Very dear. *Mahal.* But we didn't mind.
Blondies. *Susmariosep!* We were crazy
for those blondies. *Ay, naku!* "No money,
no honey," they used to say. After the war,
one time, I was going out with a blondie. She had
a white fur coat down to her feet: *maganda.*
Turned out she was some kinda Russian spy,
no kidding. The FBI haul me away
and this *puti*—blond hair, blue eyes—he comes
into the room and says, *"Kumusta kayo?"*
just like he's from Manila, and his accent's better
than mine! That time, I was working the Presidio,
folding whites in the Army hospital.
They let me go 'cause I got no top
secret to give away, you see? Believe it
or not—FBI agent talking Tagalog!

Well, I been here at the International since
long time before that blondie. I have this room
over twenty years. This same bed,
squeak squeak every night till I think
the mice are talking back. That same desk
where I used to sit and write letters back home
but I got no one there now. Same old view—
Kearny Street still the same, twenty,
thirty years. This room's all the home
I got. They kick us out, I have just one
regret: all the lotsa names I got,
no one ever called me *Lolo.* Those years
playing with blondies, I never had no kids.
And so now I can't have no grandson.
All I got is you—you college boys
ask these questions like you're doing homework.
Look around you. This is all there is.
Remember everything about this room: the smell

of old linoleum, the faded curtains,
the bugs. And when your grandkids ask about
the o.t.'s, *the* original manongs,
you tell them how we talked today. Tell them
Francisco Velarde was here. Lolo Panchito was here.

Pacific Crossing

The pier, a great concrete semicircle,
stretched into San Francisco Bay
like a father's arm around a daughter.
On Sundays, we would venture on that pier,

Mama in her broad straw hat, a country
woman in some rice paddy on Luzon.
In his lucky lime-green short-sleeved shirt, checked
by orange pinstripes, Papa would heft the net.

I would lean over the rail, watch the two
steel hoops—the smaller within the larger,
criss-crossed by heavy twine in diamond shapes—
lift out over the dark water and sink

in a green froth. A small wire cage nestled
in the center of the hoops, containing
chunks of raw meat. Papa would say, "Best bait
is porterhouse. Crabs really go for that."

Sometimes he would let me pull the net up.
The rope slimy and tight in my small hands
and then the skitter and scuttle of claws
on the wooden deck of the pier. Later

at home, I would play the radio loud, hide
that same skitter on the sides of the large
enamel-white Dutch oven, concentrate
instead on the sweetness I knew would come.

One of those Sunday evenings, I dropped in
at my friend Peter van Rijn's house. Dinner
had just been served, and the family rule
was: all the neighborhood kids had to leave.

But I didn't. There was Pete's father, like some
patriarch from a Norman Rockwell painting,
poising his carving knife above the shell—
huge and bountiful—of a red King crab.

I said, "Wait." Their heads swiveled toward me
in shock, as if I'd screamed a voodoo curse.
Old Peter, the daughter Wilhelmina, his sons—
Paul, Bruno, Guido, my friend Pete—

the Mom whose given name I never knew:
a good immigrant family. The heirs
of European culture, I always
thought, these direct descendants of Rembrandt.

I said, "Wait." And then I shared the secret
passwords to being a Filipino.
*Here is where you dig your fingernails in
to pry the top shell off. You suck this green*

*and orange jelly—the fat of the crab.
This flap on the underside tells if it's
male or female: pointed and skinny or
round like a teardrop. Here's how you twist off*

legs, pincers. Crack and suck the littlest ones.
Grip it here and here, then break the body
in half. These gray fingers are gills—chew but
don't swallow. Break the crab into quarters.

Here you find the sweetest, the whitest meat.

First Mango

For Mary Ann

Remember that June before our wedding we spent
in San Francisco? That first morning you woke
to my brother in silver sequins singing like
Diana Ross? What must have gone through your mind?
What kind of people were you marrying into?
My father who laughed a lot but was schizophrenic.
My stepmom who'd tried, they say, to stab him in the back
with scissors. Love may be blind, but not *stone* blind.

Then, one Sunday we bought at the corner market
one perfectly ripened red-gold mango.
How carefully I slit the skin with my penknife
. . . rivers of yellow juice, the furry seed . . .
then sliced the golden half-moons into quadrangles,
open petals. Your first bite of our sweet life.

VINCE GOTERA received his PhD and MFA from Indiana University. He is
the author of a book of critcism, *Radical Visions: Poetry by Vietnam
Veterans* (University of Georgia Press), and has published poems in
Kenyon Review, Caliban, Seattle Review, and *Indiana Review.* His poems
are also included in *The Open Boat* (Anchor Books, 1993).

JESSICA HAGEDORN

Souvenirs

when you don't have it
or worse yet
when you got it
n the silent woman
bathes you n feeds you
n kisses you
on behalf of yr mama n papa
n you get sent off
to the convent
for some french culture

life is cheap

in manila
where the sun is scarlet
like a beautiful slut
waiting for yr eyes
to meet hers
in the darkness;
like an indian mango
that are her lips

in manila
the women wearing veils
of black lace
on sundays
veils that smell
of sandalwood n the virgin mary

sanctity n piety

are their names
n do you remember
that pink-faced
spanish missionary
who raped my great-grandmother
when she was fourteen years old?
(i asked him if he was god)

in manila my grandmother's eye
turned blue
before dying
n her secret was revealed
like a giggle
like a slow smile
from behind handpainted
pink ivory fans
scented with jasmine
n the virgin mary
sanctity n piety
are their names
n perez prado
has a number one hit
with "patricia"
on the radio

life is cheap

igorots on horseback
n the old women
chewing betel nut
in the palengke
selling kangkong leaves
the memory of war

it's so sweet sometimes

in manila
the nuns with headdresses
like the wings of doves
piety n sanctity
are their names
n their sweet
stale n musky
in the woolen robes they wear
in the heat of a tropical day
hiding breasts n cunts
n beating you
into holy submission
with tales of purgatory
n the black saint of lima
martin de porres

n lapu lapu
was just another pagan
who cut off some spaniard's head
n magellan's statue looms instead
like a nightmare in manila
where you dream colors
of the first donald duck movie
you've ever seen
underneath a mosquito net

it's so sweet sometimes

n tito puente has a hit
n it's latin night
at the coliseum
n you don't know
these musicians
come from some place
called new york

it's just another major event
to you
a ten-year-old child
twitching her ass
n doing the cha-cha in her seat
at the coliseum

it's so sad sometimes

yr mama looking so young
n beautiful
n you can't understand
what she is
or who you are

in manila
the president's wife
dictates martial law
with her thighs
sanctity n piety
is her name
as she sips tea
in madrid

life is very cheap

Vulva Operetta

In my dream, sweaters are referred to as "vulvas." They are mohair or angora wool, of a soft, warm texture—gray, bleeding into a deep, rich red—similar to Japanese raku pottery.

We wear these sweaters.

People say things like: "It's hot. I think I'll take my vulva off."
Or: "It's cold. I think I'll put my vulva on."

Foppish men and women ask each other questions like: "Where did you
get that BEE-YOO-TEE-FULL vulva?"
Followed by remarks like:
"I think I'm gonna put my vulva in the closet. I think I'm gonna put
my vulva in the closet. I think I'm gonna put my vulva. I'm gonna. My
vulva. I."

JESSICA HAGEDORN is the editor of the acclaimed anthology of Asian American fiction *Charlie Chan Is Dead* and author of *Danger and Beauty*, a collection of selected poetry and short fiction (both published by Penguin Books in 1993). She is also the author of the novel *Dogeaters*, which was nominated for a 1990 National Book Award.

ALEJANDRINO HUFANA

The Insides of Alfred Hitchcock

Thanks to rental movies. Things I can
look over fast, they let live still. What ticks
in Hitchcock? The smug guy's film. The age was young,
he pulled the victim back—no overexposure
before her time. Not indulged, the story's fine
shocks are as chopped green onions are dropped
on shark fillet. "True to life" is all
my clockwork fellow fanciers ever say.
Blooming critics! Their likes are to do with us
the insides of Alfred Hitchcock. We stopwatch
an effect—there, a bated, shying, lean
flush of harm on Grace Kelley. Fresh, open,
cosmetiqueless herself like a peeled tender-ripe
tamarind, our fond soup condiment, relished
warm; other tastes beside are just laid on.
My wife has learned, the keeper she has been
of a house made from a turn-of-the-century
one taken down at fewer and fewer short
demands, and she tells how racked it can be
to pull an effect apart—and smear with pity.
She rolls back a goodly run of film—the climaxes
to Hitchcock's snag of nerves? No, it's deeper, the root
care for sad ends—there. It comes clean.
We've trashed heavier object blandishments
than we can keep for dear habit or virtue alone,
else parted with them as our youth but came
to this, so proved of things, our wiser scan.

From the Raw

Due the hilot, faithful to my father
and before that my grandfather through to me,
I seek his malodorous, franking cures
of root mixes with lilies of the fields.
Or shutting mimosa leaves mealed in coco oil,
or a common climbing vine minced for its sap
(at times fed the hogs before they cry hell).
Some beauty in the waste of flowers
can prove fatal. Skirt that like a sin
the hilot's grimace with the warning
still shushes on to me. It waves on thinning,
from my tried text to anything science,
waving on from essences only proved true
by mind, not anything by lab. It scents
all points, in near-muting padded crackle
mum with moss, the remains of our raw burst
into time long since. That fungal flashpoint that,
without anger as poets see such in things,
set us ordering our chaos since, collecting
as we passed poultice of stars, hilot's healing
deeper than chance, and other truths besides.
No middle way since, if need be, the hilot's
quiet parting word spreads out to bloom, I pray
in the raw rush of light and smell with earth
the limiting silence, get back as filled for a rub.

Contemporary

Potters I rose up with in a hurry
made slow things of our own ground
when proud gifts were fired outside.
Thinking them too turned within
to witness anything but dark, I hung
farther away from a common tongue
with turtles hatched more safe at sea
when I'd of saving soul have sung
as we did last of any love.

The potter's field is now officialdom
blooming with skills we never had,
only, hiring from some strange demand
potters never as faceless, on common
folded knees wanting a term to speak.
A new desert has come to cover
the race, a seedling of term in a pot
enclosed like the navel chord of old,
in meditation, carrying on in earth,
each turning fold a turn of writ,
foreclosed, just wanting to be found.

Floating Epitaphs, Their Possible Explanations in Poro Point

I.
But to end at where we came,
the washing and blowing in common,

how in the stuffing we were curled
but to flutter the flirting moths
from a decay of winding cloth.
As we wished, now an orderly world?
This I know: locked in each eye
is death by fire started there,
but cannot burn the segueing
leisure of a rounding worm.

II.
Two lie below. One brought home once
a fad of rhythm both would beat to.
The other kept to it till both forgot
they had next to right by the lot.
The lot entailed to have our more
trade places with our less, they saw
how sanguine it be alone then how
crowding it did our brute need to touch
and get mortal. Saw us half in shock
our controlled pains gone dead on
contagious joys, anew in aching
celibacy, now a tongueless indulgence
mending nothing with an unmasked skill.

ALEJANDRINO G. HUFANA has taught literature at the University of the
Philippines and is a past recipient of the Republic Cultural Heritage Award.
He has published several collections of poetry, including *Sickle Season* and
The Life of Lot and Other Poems. He lives in Long Beach, California.

April in Houston

I was familiar with the word
Magnolia
Long before I knew it was
A flower.
Where I was born, in Manila,
Magnolia
Was the trade name of our very
Best ice cream.
(In fact, my cousin was the Chief
Chemist for
The firm and thanks to him we had
Dry ice and frozen strawberries
Long before . . .
British Singapore, for instance.)

Well, only today I found out
That the word
Magnolia
Derives from Pierre Magnol, a French
Botanist
Born in sixteen-thirty-something.
Imagine!

From my bedroom window I look
Down upon
A young Magnolia tree decked in
Promises,
In soon-to-be blossoms. One more
Day and these
Will shed their inhibitions, will

Unveil their
Pale, surrealistic faces,
Issuing
Mute invitations to be kissed
Or perhaps
Inhaled. They are generous—they
Are eager
To delight any passerby.

April may well be a cruel
Month elsewhere.
Not here. April is Magnolia time!
The flowers
Sway like lanterns in the April breeze . . .
Replicas
Of unnamed, mysterious planets . . .
Or tiny
Ghosts playing house between the leaves . . .
Or could they
Be masks from some ancient drama,
Hanging there
Just waiting for the actors to
Slip them on
When lights are dimmed at curtain time?

I think I shall no longer steal
Magnolias
From the trees in Tanglewood. I've
Decided
It's a serious crime, like jewel
Theft . . . even
A kind of cruel kidnapping.

I float a magnolia in
A round, crystal bowl

And it unfolds . . .
Like a parable.

No Immunity

Lock me up. I am a
Killer. A murderer of plants.
Unwilling. Compulsive.
Far more dangerous than fire ants.
Schefflera, ivy, ferns,
Committed trustingly to me,
Are doomed. I talk to them
As equals and yet . . . R.I.P.
Maybe I'm a psycho.
M.O.'s consistent as they come.
Find the opposite of
Green. That identifies my thumb.
Premeditation's not
Involved. I don't overwater!
Hey, not Murder One, but
Involuntary Plant Slaughter.

Hope

You can't get rid of it.
I've tried everything.
The stone is a fossilized moth,

Dry as a skull in the desert.

But wait until tomorrow.

Maybe the moon does it,
The shifty fog—who cares?
The moss has spread its altar-cloth,
Inviting golden chalices.

Yes friend, yes foe of sorrow.

DOLORES DE IRURETAGOYENA DE HUMPHREY received her degree in Journalism from the University of Santo Tomas in Manila. She has published three collections of poetry, the latest being *For Sharing: Poems for Heart and Voice* (1986). She lives in Houston, Texas.

DOMINADOR I. ILIO

Marikudo in Kalibo, 1979

This is so far asea from the plateau
in Madiaas where sprawl the makeshift altars
and *barongbarongs* of the tribe.
There, every day, Polpulan tells of the rituals
of the Bisayans down the Aklan.

Long have I fancied to come and see
this spectacle, this multitude
so thick as on a barter day
in Kaguyuman. It is so animated, so frisky
as ants assaulting a spill of honey.

My wife, Maniwantiwan,
with a spray of berries in her hair
and the golden necklace of the Borneans
dangling down her front would love
to prance about and shake her buttocks
among these soot-smeared lowlanders
and tourists wriggling their bodies,
throwing up their hands, and
showing their white armpits.

But I, so black from head to toe,
feel so cooped up and alien
amidst these frenzied revelers.

We are the true Ati,
black as black can be,
sprung from the earth of Anninipay.
We are worth more than diamonds.

We are older than the Bisayans,
much older than the friars in Iloilo,
much older than the Spaniards in Manila.

Hala bira, hala bira.
Beat the gongs, ring the bells.
Hala bira, hala bira.

I will not trade my blowgun
for eight and twenty varas of nylon
nor for a wad of paper bills.

Hala bira, hala bira.
Shatter the gongs, break the bells.
Hala bira, hala bira.

Children of the Atomic Age

Down in all the plain, in the tinder-dry cities,
The prodigious children play tag and kites,
Launching into orbit in ionized
Atmosphere mathematical forms and shapes,
And in the turbid pools the paper boats.

How ruthlessly precise their bodies move,
Robotlike, arms raised as semaphores,
Peg legs as piston rods poking into
The bowels of the earth. No heart enters
Into the computed motions, not an item
Of love in the game theories. But would the parents
Spank the children? No. Far, far from it.
With rations and cameras, they'd rather scurry
Up for a weekend picnic at the summit.

Prokosch in Tehran, 1978

For N.V.M. Gonzalez

I cannot go to the bazaar
nor to the alley of the jewelers
to shop for carpets or trinkets
for souvenirs and keepsakes.

The streets are jammed with student demos
behind their makeshift barricades,
and grim-faced troopers prowl the avenues
while choppers harass the queazy air.

Bonfires tinge skyscrapers red
downtown in the row of tourist inns.
There's panic in the airline offices.
Aliens in their slept-on togs rush madly
to the airports.

But here in the suburbs
in this jaded *cravanserai*
hid by a stand of wilting alders,
refinery workmen on strike
sip leisurely their day-old bitters
unmindful of the riots.

Tonight, I will hitch a lazy ride
on a zebu cart with tinkling bells
to take me up to Tabriz.
Tuesday, I will have a quarrel
in Kazvin.

The Site of My Grandfather's House

My father once told me that as a boy
he lived in an old *mestizo* house—of wood
and thatch—some dusty kilometers from town.
Set back a goodly distance from the road,
on a rise of land, it lay hid in a grove
of trees.

    He played kites in the fields nearby,
ached with the wish to soar up with the kites
and ride the wind to see far-off horizons.
He used to shinny up the orange trees
and from the topmost branches glimpse at the sea.

Later, as a young man, he crossed that sea
and traveled many lands, but never once
returned to that old house. But talk he did,
repetitively of its arithmetic
and surrounding geography—the girth and height
of the posts, the many rooms, the termite mounds
that yielded mushrooms after a night of thunders,
the *kakawate* fence, and the sandstone outcrops—
down the slope to the spring that never dried up.
He loved that house and loved to tell about it,
each fervid telling bringing new architecture
and ghosts to the house.

    And so the homestead became
a splendid country estate in my dreams,
with winding lanes under silvery orange trees
and sculptured angels along the sunlit byways.

In time, I crossed the unfamiliar sea

to end my errant father's odyssey.
I braved the *aswangs* and the one-eyed *sigbins*
just to see the site of Grandpa's house.

A freshly gravelled road and then the hillock
—so overgrown with weeds, and yet so bare.
Unfenced, albino goats despoiled the grounds.
I traced a path that led to a grassy hollow;
the cleft on the layered rock had healed, but still
a teary trickle seeped into the dirt
and kept the basin damp. Up on the knoll,
a carpet of green defined the house's geo-
metry and on one corner stood, good lord,
a tall, disfigured totem pole.

                    Tear-eyed,
I scratched the muck around, hoping to find
a shard of pottery, a colored bead—
oh, any legacy from my forebears.
But all that turned up was clean, sticky clay.
And I choked. For I had found, and held
in my hands the sterile soil, the cruel earth
that drove my father on his wanderings.

DOMINADOR I. ILIO was born in 1913 in Malinao, Aklan. During World
War II he fought against the Japanese with the guerillas led by Col.
Macario Peralta, Jr. From 1952 to 1954 he worked on his MA in Hydraulics
at the State University of Iowa and while there attended the renowned
poetry workshop of Paul Engle where he befriended Donald Justice, W.
D. Snodgrass, and William Stafford. His latest book is *Madia-as,* a novel
in verse about the indigenes of Panay.

JAIME JACINTO

Tongue Tied

Being tongue tied is what
they liked to teach you
inside the classroom
when the young priests
spoke only in English.

So here is what happened
on the first day of school
when you spoke like your
mother and father—
a taboo of syllables spilling
from your tongue until
teacher's ruler reddened
your knuckles.

On the second day
it is your turn again
because you whispered
Putang Ina Mo. You must pass
a test of time and balance,
standing alone in a corner,
a New Testament in each hand.

You do not look when they fall
from your outstretched arms
but listen instead to the cries
filling the cloakroom dark
as the man called Brother
slaps your bare ass.

A reminder for all who could hear
of the rule you had to follow
and the language we could not speak.

On the third day,
it is someone else's turn.
Inside the boy's lavatory a classmate
tells his version of Goldilocks
who returned to her province
riding in a jeepney. And beside her
sat four bears instead of three.
So who were they? went the riddle.

We named three but did not
know the last until he answered
naming them one by one.
Papa bear, mama bear, baby bear,
and of course *"der was da driber."*

Our laughter ends when Brother enters
and lifts the riddler into a trash bin.
There he'll stay, Brother says, until
he learns to speak properly
in this classroom where words
burned silent in our tongues.

Heaven Is Just Another Country

I'm going to die, he says
not to anyone in particular,
it's the sting of bitterness
he's talking to and at

142

the head of the table
in a Chinatown restaurant
he orders another scotch
before dinner.

With mother shaking her head,
I help him
from his chair to the john.
He pees slowly
fingers like knobby roots
on his fly, passing a test
of agility for a man this drunk.

I'm dousing cold water on his forehead
and he tells me again he's dying,
Don't say a word to your mother
about this and please forget
you ever saw me this way.

I pretend not to hear,
unaccustomed to the openess
and instead, remember how
you were once a young man
new to America where you learned
to drive a Plymouth sedan
back and forth to work every day,
to sit at a desk chainsmoking
and drawing blueprints for
the houses you never saw.

I want to be seven again
and ride with you on the early morning streets
down Market St. across Sixth and Brannan, and beyond
to your desk of scattered papers,
to an ashtray piled with cigarette stubs.

But back home, I watch you slump
into an armchair and sigh
from the whiskey that pinches your swollen waist.
Tonight, you say, *heaven is just another*
country and the trip begins
within an airplane like the one you rode
30 years back,
with propellers spinning
so fast you forget
you are in America
inside your living room
and instead,
you are singing at the top of your lungs
like your own son beside you
because far below there is nothing
but blue tide and an ocean crossing.

Absence

No longer with us, you are that man I once feared,
when whiskey filled your words until what we heard
became our own silence. So if I were to think of you now
with a love grown from that fear, you'd be the man who
brought food to our table with a glass of whiskey
to cool his wrinkled brow. You'd be that man
and I his son who sat in silence.

And if we spoke then, it was to say let us not talk
of our love or of your dying. I can hear you even now
home from the office, climbing the basement stairs
grocery bags hanging from each speckled hand.
Let's talk if at all, about the weather,

the lottery ticket you kissed for good luck,
and have you heard the latest box scores?
All those small words greeting the silence
that lived among us.

Visitation

It is spring today
and I think of him
kneeling beside me
this companion
who was my father's father,
who appeared one day
and stayed with us,
never to leave the house—
all day dressed in pajamas
shuffling in his slippers
down the back stairs
to the garden where we'd watch him
bunching the dead leaves
tamping the pulpy soil
flicking the hollow shells of dead beetles.
He would tend his garden
day by day, little by little
brushing away the loose earth,
the soggy crumbs of moss
until his fingers found
what they had wanted.
From a fist full of black earth—
the pale green sprouts
more delicate than morning light.

Now years later when I'm nearly asleep
listening to the slow movements
of animals, the rustle of leaves
where their paws might fall,
he returns, ancient, waving
his leathery hands,
knuckles nicked by thorns.
I hear him whispering
our names, and the night breeze passes
over us with the first sliver of moonlight.

JAIME JACINTO's poetry has appeared in various anthologies, includ-
ing *Without Names* (Kearny Street Workshop Press, 1985), *Breaking
Silence* (Greenfield Review Press, 1983), and *Premonitions* (Kaya
Productions, 1995).

FATIMA LIM-WILSON

Alphabet Soup
(Mimicry as a Second Language)

*A*ngel of letters, feed me.
*B*eat your wings till I remember
*C*ardboard cut-outs of ABCs. Why
*D*oes my memory hobble, lift
*E*mpty pails from an English castle's dark well?
*F*ill me with the welter of vowels,
*G*oogol of consonants, tender French
*H*earts, dead Latin roots from where words grow,
*I*nsidiously. My tongue smokes, a
*J*oss stick trailing mixed signals. What
*K*eeps me from balancing a silver spoon
*L*ocked in my mouth? An echo.
*M*other humming her made-up melodies. She
*N*udges me to move my lips with hers.
*O*ld wives rustle, whisper tales in my ears.
*P*alimpsest of long-tailed syllables,
*Q*uick darting wings of a wind-seeking accent.
*R*un, I must rend the tent of Thesaurus.
*S*lash away till I warble, silvery voiced with a cut
*T*ongue. I grow, a hunchback, trailing my master,
*U*nctuous and anxious. Sweet, mute angel, cast your
*V*eil over me to muffle my voice of broken glass.
*W*ith your flaming sword, mark me, with a bloody
X to form my lips into singing, always, a heartfelt
*Y*es. Spewing baubles, I become the favored one. In this
*Z*oo of sycophants, I'm the parrot who's almost human.

The Beginning of Things

Tonight, we make up our own legends.
As we go along we discover
Buried treasure. Why, when
Touched, does skin raise rows
Of budding flowers, a castle,
Lightning shows? Did you hear
Of the two lovers too entwined
They made the gods so jealous
They had to spend their entire lives
Aching for each other, one turned
Into a rock, the other a bay?
Only, for a few minutes each day
With the tide could they, with rage
And mad laughter, embrace. And so
I recall their tragedy in the midst
Of our pleasure, taking even more
Time to name and rename the sudden
Dip between the waist and hip,
The regions where lips rest most
At home. I conjure up a full
Moon, chant a forbidden word
Three times, and stir in our
Bed, a pool in whose clear water
I see our future. Kingdom
Of locked limbs, shared breath.
The answers now come flying
Like a winged horse or gold coins
Spilling from a magic purse.
Barefoot, I dance through fire.
I tower over trees. And I bring
To you, still smoking and warm,
The beggar hands of a goddess.

Ringmaster's Wife

You jerk me,
A circus animal in chains,
And my mind suspends tightropes.
I perform on automatic pilot
Doing cartwheels, doing house
Chores, twirling balanced meals
On broom handles, pulling laundry,
Pressed and ironed, out of my sleeves
With the bravura of the hard
Muscled ballerina. Under the hot
Glare of your wordless commands,
My senses reel, blindly tracking down
The sweetness of the invisible carrot.

* * *

Sometimes, you take me out for walks.
I blink in the sun, stiff
In my comical hats and striped suits.
Your friends approve, they throw
Crumbs, loose change. Offer silence
Of the one hand's applause. They praise
You for the diamonds in my eyes.

* * *

At night, my dreams pace. Fly over
The big top. I no longer plan escapes.
As you drunkenly throw daggers, never
Missing the heart, I crawl out
Of reach, finding a warm spot
In the darkness of your silken hat,
Between the crooning doves.

* * *

Raising the Dead

> "At least 120 people died when a floating shrine
> sank in the Bocaue River. Police officer Sonny Pablo said
> those aboard the boat were singing and praying . . ."
>
> —*Philippine News* report, July 1993

Wreath-heavy, a child's body
Glistens in the sun, cruciform
Among many whose limbs swell
With significance: Last
Breath arrested in grace,
Still singing of Mary's
Embrace of the broken sacrifice
That was her son. His cross
Sprouted from these waters.
This they believe as firmly
As they grip its ragged bark
Swaying upon the shrine.
One touch and tumors melt away,
Lost fortunes turn up in rice pots,
And wandering husbands, remembering
Home, break into a run.
Just as the bleeding woman
In that jostling crowd seared
Christ's hem with the fervor
Of her passing fingers,
Their faith lightnings through
The sacred wood. His love
Too much to bear knocks them
Down, down into depths of joy,
The blue robes of an upturned sky.
Their ears ring with their own
Exultance. Their bodies drag new wings.

FATIMA LIM-WILSON teaches at Shoreline Community College in Seattle, Washington and is the author of, *Wandering Roots/From the Hothouse,* which won a Colorado Book Authors Award in 1991 and a Manila Critics' Circle National Book Award in 1992. Her book of poems *Crossing the SnowBridge* won the *Journal* Award in Poetry and was published by Ohio State University in 1995. She is a recipient of a Pushcart Prize in poetry and her poems have appeared widely in u.s. journals such as *Kenyon Review, Prairie Schooner,* and *Bomb.*

MICHAEL MELO

Unlearning English

is slow. Tedious. Like midnight mass on Christmas Eve.
The mating of tortoises. The struggle with strands
of jumbled phonics, hybrids of "*Hoy,* how are you,"
half-remembered *tsismis,* gossip from Grandma.
There are times when my tongue is ready to burst,
all synapses to language are gone
and I understand what happened
at Babel. Each sentence I speak is
a taffy pull.

My cousins have a field day with my Tagalog.
They have a saying
for me: I am "He-who-can-speak-
with-infants." And so our lessons begin,
the wringing of my tongue.

A
Not "ay." Ah. *Adobo.*
Ang pagod natin. All this effort
makes me ache—why did I forget?

B
Why weren't the words burned
in my brain? B. The sheep
says "ba." *Bawal umihi dito.*
Don't break *balut* on the wall.
Boiled duck embryo in leathery shell,
it smells bad. It is also bad
to forget where you came from.

K

There is no c in Tagalog.
Kah, ka. No-ka.
Kahit ano man, whatever the cost,
ka-kainin ko ang kaong,
I will eat the candied coconut seed.

D

Da-da fed mama *duhat* while I was in the womb.
That is why I am so dark.

E

Every phrase I make sounds stupid,
overkill. Each sentence is
unwieldy and clumsy, a pig's house
made of twigs. Eh. Eh.
Eng-ot. Why did you forget?

G

In the beginning, gah. Go.
Ga-go. *Gago,* fool, gago.
You are *gago.* Very good.
In the beginning it is all the bad words
that you learn first.
Gago. Good.

H

Ha. Haba. How long
has it been since I felt the harness
of language around my head?
The taste of a Tagalog heaven
to me, whose sense of country has been long
replaced by *Hogan's Heroes.*
Happy Days.

I
I. No, eee. *Ingat,*
careful. In the Manila wind
you may find a mosquito and
itch all night. Itch, itch.
Oh, Mother! *Ay, inay!*

M
My mother remembers all this, and more.
Ma. Mango—*manga!* The unripe manga
dipped in *bagoong*
unwaters the mouth.

N
Nanu Ken wa? What's going on?
The sounds are right
but the words are all wrong.
A half-remembered song.

Ng
Nga, bagoong, the many watching eyes
like those in brown jars
of the salted shrimp fry.

O
Oh, *bahay kubo,* little house
with thatched roof of bamboo,
the kind that Lolo lived in
while growing gardens of *upo* and *santol.*

P
Pa. Papa. *Pancit canton,*
the noodles that Papa cooks
at each party. Proverb, Papa-style:
the poor and the rich will gladly

sit & eat with you, even your own
brothers and sisters will stick
their hands in your pockets and pick
your wallet while you laugh.

R
It is easier to write about the Philippines
than forget who is still there. Uncle Romy
and his shrill police whistle, his son,
Romualdo who swore to kill his father
if he ever left his mother for another.

S
Sa Bayan, at the supermarket
I learned just how slow my tongue is.
In the time it takes me to compose a sentence,
a man, sibilant, sells his old wheelbarrow
and two gray chickens, while a freak storm
begins and ends. He lunched on *suman* sweetened
with white sugar, wrapped in a sheath
of wet banana leaves.

T
Tatay, Father, Ta-tie, try to understand
that you did teach me much.
You taught me that the only thing
I needed to know was where I came from,
and not to go back.

U,W,Y
Usok, smoke from the cigarette
of a tattooed man *ubod nang libag*
rises to the black circle
that halos Manila. Near Clark
Air Force Base, a street

where whores are as plentiful
as rain, where any day you may die
from guerillas while on a *kalesa* to Luneta—
you remember your voice
because you are American
because you are a dark Pilipino-American
and that they will *balisong* your tongue
because they can tell you speak
unlearned English.

Red Lipstick on a Straw

For Tess Gallagher

There was a plastic cup of iced coffee
out in the open on Debbie's desk
with a straw brown on the inside from
coffee seeping back to the cup,
and on top of the straw was a strawberry red smudge,
and all day I am fixating on this image.
Maybe it's the red lipstick on the straw
or just the idea of lipstick,
red as a Coca-Cola commercial
sticking on the lips of one who has been kissed
from one who did the kissing.
A kiss is just one mouth touching another
nothing more, nothing less,
but I get all red thinking about it.
I never see Pilipinos kiss much,
at least my parents don't in front of other people,
and when they do, it's half-hearted,
more giggling and blushing

than a leaning into the kiss
and really living it.
The last time I saw them kiss was 1992,
in August, it was their silver anniversary
and when the priest said "You may kiss the bride,"
the people in the Church, they were mostly Pinoys,
were laughing. My father's back had
given out from all the kneeling and he was
a little stiff, and he gave my mom a stiff kiss,
her eyes opened wide as her mouth closed,
and people laughed. I thought,
gee it's a kiss, that's 25 years of kissing
right there. The laughing was loud and so I thought,
maybe they haven't kissed
for 25 years. Maybe it's only 10. Or 5.
I've never known. When I asked,
they said, "Kisses, to Pinoys,
are to be behind closed doors.
It's shameful to kiss out in public.
Like loving, kisses should be quiet
so no one else hears or knows."
But I never really knew whether their
kisses were quiet or maybe
there were no kisses at all,
just dark closed doors at night and only the glow
of TV kissing.

I like the sound of real kissing.
To me it means loving going on.
I know it feels good to be kissed
when I want a kiss. I remember my first one,
lying on Sheila's bed, listening
to Eponine sing "A Little Fall of Rain"
and watching Sheila look at me and wonder why I
was all of a sudden holding her hand.

My hand was warm,
it has always been warm, and my cheeks were hot
even though the Berkeley wind through her
fourth floor window blew cold air
between us. I stared into Sheila's brown eyes,
her cheeks were reddening too,
a hawk moth fluttered by in slow motion
and everything was going
blurry. Sheila's lips were slick and greasy
from the butter popcorn we shared
and it made our kissing easy,
I had only to raise my head six inches because she
too was feeling kissable. It was five seconds
of closed-eyes, lips on greasy lips,
five seconds of heaven
it was my first kiss, a falling-in-love kiss,
it was a James Brown screaming "Hit Me,
I Feel Good" kind-of-kiss.

God I want another one.
I want one now, I've been wanting one
the whole day. I am lonely, my lover is faraway
and probably wants a kiss as well,
or has made herself busy to not want one.
I get a little crazy thinking of that,
Sheila boxing herself in her room,
closing her door and busying herself to not want
a kiss, or not think of wanting one.

This 5 months and 3000-mile distance between us
makes me curl my toes into my mocha rug
all the more while my fingers pull at my hair
or squeeze pillows for tears.
I am told it's cute to see me
miss her and write poems on missing her

kisses, but I don't want sympathy.
I want her home.
Yesterday I was in my car driving past
Buena Vista at sunset, watching a couple
jog to the stoplight in their matching
blue-and-purple sweats. They stood there,
talking with their hands on their hips,
shaking away the aches from their legs.
The red-headed woman stood on her tiptoes,
reached up,
and hugged her man,
leaned into him
and kissed him
and as she kissed him,
I opened my mouth
and closed my eyes,
and for five seconds
ignored the horns behind me.

Scrambled Eggs and Garlic Pork

Sheila and I spent the night talking about French.
I've always thought French to be such a sexy language
and yet how awful my French became as I tried
more and more to woo her with cool Frenchy words—
"voulez vous couches avec fromage sussois"
did not make the hair on the back of her neck
stand like *"Kumain ka na. Meron kanin at adobo
dito."* It's funny, I don't remember much
Tagalog, I've lost it the way sex
transforms a virgin to another Joe Schmoe

in the crowd. And yet Sheila says no, she says
I am still very much Pilipino even if I choose
not to believe it. And she says even a white girl
like her can tell I'm the real thing
by the way her legs grind tight together—
she purrs on the phone
when I speak of browned scrambled eggs and garlic pork,
and how we should clean the toilet,
"Mag linis tayo nang kubeta ngayon," she finds it sexy
and I'm thinking god, her pale legs are rubbing
together, they are making more heat than we ever did,
I find this out now, when she is in Boston,
I find this out now, she was here the whole summer
on my blue bed in my apartment, not once did
our hips meet, and yet now I can count
from *isa* to *tatlong-po,* and slowly drag my
vowels, *isa, dalawa, tatlo, apat, lima,*
anim, and count her sighs and heaves,
and shit goddamn
why did I
forget so much?

I think of my father as I twist these words
for good phone, I remember his black tape player
on his desk. And after he'd been cutting hearts
and livers and tongues from Vienna Sausage
he always brought home these thick
textbooks and every night he would *kalong*
my brother on his lap, and together they would
learn how to pronounce English correctly.
I would go to bed and see the light underneath
my door, and go to sleep listening to
my father spit his FS & PS on the table.
Fair. Few. Finger. Fat. Frogs. Fire.
Pumice. Polka. Pat. Pitted Prunes.

We didn't have FS in our alphabet.
When he'd get confused and say *"Fark,"* people would laugh,
especially the folks at work, those Polish
and German Americans, they were merciless at
the butcher shop. My father, degreed and educated
in Luzon was just another cow to be punched around,
each day I could tell when he came home
another man made fun of his tongue, it just wouldn't
go the right way today, or yesterday, or tomorrow.
Few and fine and park and pickle and five and fuck,
they were only words but they meant the difference
between not good and never good enough in America.

And me? Here I am, figuring out how to woo
and woo my love to bed tonight and I bet
if we could, my father and I would slice tongues
and trade in an instant.

MICHAEL MELO's poems are published in *ZYZZYVA* and *Spillway*. He is currently a systems engineer for Time-Warner Interactive in Burbank, California. On August 23, 1996, he will have married the *Sheila* of his love poems.

NOEL MATEO

There Is No Word for Sex in Taglog

look it up
you won't find it anywhere
it's not in the dictionary
instead—metaphors for the unspoken
euphemisms blinding enlightenment

implied in its mystery
something comes close
a word of the streets
where sex was thought to belong—
whisper *kantotan* in their ears
with mischief in your eye
guilt, maybe shame

the *titi* and the *puki*
spoken in adolescent murmurs
sex in the shadows
assumed knowledge
repressed and pretended
to be there but never spoken of

talong the long eggplant
dark purple smooth phallic
saging ni pasing
ITT CO MAKATI
ang titi ko malaki
you wish

mani and cherry
who's afraid of vagina cool

hidden underneath the *saya*
all covered in guilt
why you so afraid of it

Filipina the *mahinhin*
Pinoy must be *lalaki*
he who must wear the pants
after all these years
still a Catholic colony

you had to have done it sometime
too many of you
for immaculate conceptions
or sitting on public toilets
so give it a name
call it wonderful
God's gift to you
you beautiful and tragic tongue

Jeepneyfying

there you go again
lowering that Dodge Colt
must be in the blood
turning anything on wheels into a jeepney
buying rims at Price Club
a Blaupunkt deck with the ultimate Alpine Amp
speakers costing more than the car itself

there you go again
tinting all your windows

getting stopped in Oakland
you're too dark
your winshield or your skin
he didn't say
there you go again
putting on that spoiler
who you think you are
Filipino Al Unser
I'll answer dat
my other car is also a piece of shit
friends don't let friends drive
hyundais
signifying through jeepneyfying

your dad bought a van
he couldn't leave it alone
hung a rosary on the rearview mirror
Baclaran candle on the dash
six lace curtains on the windows
seashells all around

bumper to bumper
full of disneyland stickers
small world you see
hologram of magic mountain
shallow grand canyon is deep very deep
tahoe and vegas—dreams of hitting it big
very superstitious
blessed by father Pol
covered his plastic rear seats
steered the wheel with imitation leather

there he goes again
backing up
annoying the neighbors

164

tweet tweet tweet like a garbage truck
announcing the arrival
I shall return macarthur
jeepneyfying to signify

NOEL MATEO was educated at the University of California and Yale University. He lives and works in San Diego, California.

CLOVIS L. NAZARENO

Bohol's Tarsier Population

We are not as small as we appear to be.
When we do make an appearence,
we come in camouflage.
Palm-small, but forest meaningful.

Older than the farthest reach of memory,
we have four hands to stun your perception,
we have huge eyes to shame your conscience,
we are endangered like your civility.

We leap from one bush to another,
insects scarcely surviving
our elemental hunger. Your primal fear—
that one day your forest fur

shall perish in one big planetary explosion
when we cease to be small and primate,
when we become an ingredient of a big black statement.
We mean more than our size.

The Cortes Swamp

The river swells onto the flooded banks;
a fog of sorrow hovers over the face;
we have sweet marsh reeds for lashes.

Vast is the hectare of our life
bounded by watersheds of mountains
and corridors of sea; we are enclosed

terrestrially. Swamp is our system.
Hair grows sinisterly into heart-shapes.
Lobsters and crabs pinch our smiles

to craft the low-points of our life.
Mangroves watch over the riverbanks
marking the perimeter of water's freedom.

But skyward there is no limit
to our sneezing; on this, my thirty-third
year, I am the seagull with the cold,

dreams shivering, contemplating
our vast fixture.
To disengage after a cough and a blink—

the river below pulling me down into mud.

CLOVIS L. NAZARENO is a Palanca Memorial awardee and has attended
the University of the Philippines and Silliman University Writer's
Workshop. He currently works as Project Director of the Bohol People's
Art Development Center. He lives with his wife and three children in
Moto Sur, Loon, on the enchanting island of Bohol in the Philippines.

YOLANDA PALIS

Waking Up

Book reviews . . .
that's how it
all began.
in 1969/
nearly a year
after
Paris, 1968.
Revolt/resistance
c'était la mode,
à l'epoch.

At home it was
moral
slowly waking up
to corruption,
bribery and murder . . .

elections coming up!
another chance
for change.
C'mon, we need to participate.

Sartre/de Beauvoir
radical
it was the trend.
Police at the
State University
was a novelty—
even with bureaucrats
                    and fascists—

we thought it was romantic.
Then Sammy missed an appointment.
Buddy was rumored as missing.
Residences were raided for
what? Uzzis, I suppose.
I learned to hide
first, to save my own—
then others.
The habit sticks.
I am
reviewing books again.

The Floor

was dirt
packed solid.
Walls of
bamboo, cut
in half, lengthwise.

A bed of bamboo
slats; rough
sofa for
the day—bed
when dark.

I remember most the
reek:
a mixture of cooked
rice,

rancid oil, and pungent
dried sweat.

A comforting room:
when distressed
I escaped
from heartless
handling.

At school, I heard
parents love their
young. I know
this is not so.

They claim to love—
instead I was eaten raw.

Yolanda Palis left the Philippines to study in Paris, France and upon graduation, came to work in Washington, DC. Her poems have been published in the Philippines and in France and she is the author of a collection of poetry, *Various Times* (1993).

PATRICK PARDO

Untitled

i was on the couch when the jehova's witnesses came.
asleep. one day after halloween.
there were two of them. one woman, one man.
he in beige suit from sears, she in white
and black.
she did all the talking. he held the screen door
open.
i nodded my head between quotes from the new testament,
she looked me in the eye and i watched the traffic,
waiting for something to happen.
everlasting life, she kept saying, everlasting life.
she showed me a picture of paradise.
it was in color.
i was very much relieved to know this.
to know that eternal life will be like she said,
like the picture, like it is outside the door now—
green and yellow. blue. and orange.
i said thank you to them. told them i would
remember what they said.
and then i went back to sleep on the couch—
the red one with the good springs.

PATRICK PARDO was born in Kansas in 1969. He was educated at Vassar and Sarah Lawrence College and his poems appear regularly in journals such as *420*. He lives and works in New York City.

BINO A. REALUYO

The Sojourners

The surrounding boxes alarm you
because now you know they're
not empty anymore. You slowly fill
them with life's selected tangibles:
black-and-white photographs,
clothing you'd soon outgrow
and crumbs of moments never consumed,
all in a rush to be claimed.
The rose-colored dress you wore
when he betrayed you is folded
on one side. The ones that carried
his scent of loyalty are placed
in the middle, preserved like the
dried fish hanging at the window,
its shadow cast for breakfast.
You are thinking of your children,
who themselves rummage through
the house, selecting certain things
for a few boxes, maybe also picking
the ones that will bring a mouthful
of smiles, leaving the rest
to be shipped to the past, in a trunk
walled with scratches of violent hours.
Together, you all wait for a whole day's
trip to the uncertain.
A new land with so much expectation
tilling your empty stomachs.
Tomorrow, all the many years
you fit in these boxes, you'll
unpack for the coldest years ahead.

La Querida

The browning of leaves
was never so prolonged as now.
Under an Acacia tree,
where soil once hid stealthily
from the sun,
you used to wrap your hands around mine,
eating salted eggs from my fingers,
burying the shells with yours,
like a root
as if to sprout
on the clay when we return to this very spot
for the naming of an unborn child.

Weeks soon became months.
The depression on this ground
has since leveled except
for this part
where my waiting rested so deeply
with remnants of stolen time.
Now marked by an unusual growth of plant.
You have returned to your wife.
(And so I have been told.)

All I see here is sun,
which was all you left for me
and this full moon I carry
predicting the coming of a storm.
On this dirt that I dig,
I am reliving our ceremony
of eggshells, kneeling
on broken twigs and lies—
like I would on your wife's face,

searching for thumbprints, a name
a strand of your curly black hair,
anything and anything
to give a newly-born son.

Bino A. Realuyo was awarded a Van Lier Fellowship in Creative Writing from the Asian American Writers' Workshop in 1993. He lives in New York City.

DANTON R. REMOTO

Exile

After my reading
he comes to me—
an old man with hair
like white waves—
telling me about "the p.i."
where he lived briefly
after the war.

"Your people, they always smile.
Is the Manila Hotel still there?
Ah, the heat,
how can I forget the heat?"

Outside, spring has already wakened
everything.
But still I shudder
(how long will the cold wind blow?),

Each of us straining our eyes,
craning our necks,
listening to the swell
and foam of faraway voices.

To each, his own version,
of those islands burning
in the sun.

Rain

This morning, it is raining
in my country.
Water slides down
the leaves,
like tongue on skin.
The sound of their falling
collects
like breath on the lobes
of ears.

You are a continent
away.
There the leaves
are now beginning
to turn.
Soon night will steal hours
from day,
and snow will be whirling
in drifts.

But you are here,
in the country
of my mind,
wiping away the maps
of mist
on the windowpane,
lying in bed beside me,
as the pulse of pillows and sheets,
even the very throb of rain,
begins to quicken.

Black Silk Pajamas

For Zack

Those black silk pajamas
become you.

They began with worms
spinning filaments
from their very lips,

Then woven into cloth
by the most delicate
of hands.

Mirrors gleam
darkly
from the pajamas'

Most secret
folds,
while I stand

Before you,
astonished
at the sight

Of so much pure
black water
rippling over your body

Like a wave or a caress.

Images of John (1967-92)

For Vida

I.
These are what I will remember:
John writing a story
about a temple in Nepal,
the monks walking in the predawn chill—
the road dipping and rising—
their hands clasped together
as if protecting a flame
from the wild wind blowing.

II.
The three of us strolling,
the leaves listening
to our every footfall,
then you holding my hand,
telling me
you have found him.
Your eyes hold him in:
John walking in the morning sun,
a song filling his every vein.

III.
I sit silently
during your marriage ceremony.
My words to myself
fall like pebbles:
How hard it is
to find somebody
who will open windows and doors

to let you in.
I remember the days
of our growing up—
pages alternately bright and black—
and I run to you,
my voice grainy.

IV.
It is winter:
The chill resides in my bones.
I open your letter smelling of home,
and I see his photograph
with your first child:
"You should have been his godfather,"
you wrote, "if only you were here."
John holds her
tightly, lovingly.
In his eyes, wonder
at his daughter—
his skin, blood, hair
brushing against him beautifully,
suddenly.

DANTON R. REMOTO received postgraduate degrees in Literature from
Ateneo de Manila University and in Publishing Studies from the
University of Stirling in Great Britain. He is currently teaching English at
the Ateneo de Manila University. His poems have been published in
Bomb and *Frank,* and a collection of his poetry, *Skin Voices Faces,* was
published by Anvil in 1991. He is the coeditor (with J. Neil C. Garcia) of
Ladlad: An Anthology of Philippine Gay Writing.

AL ROBLES

Feasting with Etang a Hundred Times Around

Three blue king
salmon-heads
A five-pound
freshwater catfish
Thrown into a pot
Sliced down the middle

The taste of ancestral cooking
Travels back a thousand years
Nothing really changed
Only the clothes in america
Etang ran barefoot in the philippines
Her tribal spirit rose forever strong
What did my mother, etang, leave behind?
What does a young mind remember?
Coming here to america when she was only 18
Waterbuffaloes still roam the countryside
Christian missionaries cling on to minds like dead flies
The *dalaga* sprouts up like wild grass
Out of the muddy rice fields
The *hito* feed on rotting flesh in the cemeteries
The pasig river piled high with garbage
Tondo smells of death
The poor get lost in the emptiness of the rich
The Malacañang palace stands still like
A dead penis pissing in a dead river
Flooding every canal and street and valley
The little priests and nuns and bishops
And archbishops carry on a four hundred year long
Tradition of indoctrination & enslavement & oppression.

remembering the past

i have lived
so far
so much
knowing their lives
living in the same rooms
as small as teapots
in j-town
in chinatown
in manilatown
the old flats
converted
broken up
into individual rooms
tiny kitchens
concentration camps
after the war
they came back home
in the sadness of
a thousand winter snows
they can fill my mind
remembering
when i was only 10 years old
i knew them all
by their first name
the erection of all day thinking
stretched block after block
the prostitutes
one story high
every face & dimple
creased my mind
i saw terry, the madam
as the shades were pulled

down & a white man
ran upstairs—
looking back

a hundred thousand
snowcrane diaries
deep scars
in their hearts
torn spirits
yet and yet
the songs, the dreams
are still alive
poems of a thousand autumn leaves
nihonmachi
the karita-sans
the kume-sans
the sato-sans
how i remember them
in my childhood days
how i remember them now
j-town
manilatown
chinatown . . . is my life.

and in j-towns
i knew them all
the old, the young
the corner grocer
heavy rain poems
waka tanka poems
break loose
in the nihonmachi wind
next door to pilipino town
pilipino barbershops
sitting there

on a little stool
how i remember having
my hair cut
the sound
of my youth & the chattering
of pinoys in the background
and the fresh smell of manju
coming from Benkyodo's pastry shop
buchanan & geary street
criss-crossing my mind

street traveling
from manju
to daikon
to bancha
to bop city
listening to
"there'll never be another you"
to manilatown
& back again
to chinatown
all over again
inside every room—
strong smell of incense
facing a brick building
old hands in mine
a thousand flowers

in the streets
the bloods ran
fighting against white boys
up the hill
downhill
in the marina & northbeach
when all was white

fell over
a large pig
next door
to the iloilo center
the circle of brown
on buchanan & ellis street
down the block from fillmore
two blocks from j-town
a hidden backyard
pilipino ritual
where a white man's eyes
never touched
gone forever
passed away
in the forgotten dreams
kept alive in a poem
and the streets crowded with blacks

Cutting Back the Ifugao Past

Heading over to Bulaan Alaaga's
The tribal past pushes far back
How could anyone remember
Twenty centuries back
What could he remember?
Wild boar racing uphill
Thru mountain mist & fog
Who knows this place called
Ifugao mountain?
Hunting deer over the ridge
With his brother

What did he leave behind?
Mountain rice terraces hung
Like jewels from the gods
WHO DANCES TO THE RICE GODS
WHO DANCES TO THE RICE GODS
Nothing here is really forgotten
Everything is recorded
In the northern part of his mind
Bulaan Alaaga's spirit stretches
Far back to the mountain-sky gods
To down-river-up-river gods
Who could tell where the river stops?
Left ifugao mountain a long time ago
Ended up at the international hotel.

The Manong with a Thousand Tribal Visions

S.F. homebound kearny street
Gray clouds hung thick
Over brown Luzon skin
Sheen from Mindanao coconut oil
Sliding smoothly across the
Taxi dance floors of America
In polished florshiem shoes

Wild pig visions run
Ifugao rain forest
Bagobo dreams rise up
Screaming for carabao urine
To irrigate the manong rice fields
Igorot coconut visions flow

Luzon river tales twirl round
In the mouth of a carabao
Tiptoe to the edge of manilatown

AL ROBLES was born in s.f. ifugao mountain—in a place called manila
town where the smell of chicken blood fills the air—where adobo soaks
up your tribal vision—where pig entrails dangle like rosary beads from
the sky—where carabaos dance on each rice grain—where the taste of life
is in the heart of fish tales and lioncloth rituals—where brown hands
meet the moon together.

E. SAN JUAN, JR.

The Owl of Minerva Takes Flight in the Evening

Mephistopheles loquitur in propria persona:

I, E–S–J–, poet by vocation, now make my first will and
testament before hired goons gun me down for my incendiary verse
that has spawned assassins. Before Manila burns down, I bequeath
to you my name stolen from the Madrid directory when our Walled
City was but one virginal pigsty. I give you the dithyrambic
sweat of my armpits as I receive in turn the ordure from your huge
cloaca of respectable virtues and pieties: antiseptic bliss
spewed out from Vatican sewers. A fair exchange.

Let me go naked with my thousand-year-old Indio hide that would
shame all flagellants *(hombre, soy desengaño)* and all propagandists
who suffer their father's death—Party slogans stink! Language
goes down the drain. Addressing the moonstruck hoi polloi
blind mouths commune with their million-volt ideals
while bankers hoard dictionaries in prostitutes' navels and
call girls cry in the wilderness from Escolta to Makati.
Well, perhaps I'm guilty of not shifting my bones and intestines
to the wanderings of your nebulae, catching comets and meteors
by stereoscope radar in my groin. My nerves, exposed to stellar
radiations, cannot decipher visions of death's iconography.

Mrs. Orgullo, real estate broker, flushes the cash register down
the w.c. with all metaphors and symbols usury has acquired
in the bargain. But I begin from scratch, inscribing curses
on your altars and disintegrating all esthetique into muck.
(Hombre, soy desengaño) Catharsis? But Rembrandt's burghers
heard pigs squeal in the slaughterhouse while primadonnas,
thrice-aborted sugarmommies, titillate the eardrums of our
financial experts whose vaults bulge with infants' guts . . .

187

and those bastards, ah, the stupid poor rushing to the Finland
Station, pouring their blood to idols who devour them—

You say this nihilism's a dead end, a cul de sac? Well and good.
There's always a need for Euphrates, since fungus and mold
has embalmed our wits before the menopause of dummies and
mannequins. I, poet-prestidigitator, offer TNT to our economic
czars (if they're not yet extinct) whose slide rules prod
the profit-motive engine toward a booming apocalypse.
Forgive us, the only purge needed is suicide on a one hundred
percent interest.

I, E–S–J–, 29 years old, declare myself sick of all god-kissing
carrions and this versifying rut—Let's join that gun-runner
in Abyssinia—what's his name? Axe that piano! Iron shovels
will smash your precious Victorian bric-a-brac. Let the
Madonna of the estero and the Virgin of affluence market
this pulp for wrapping rotten fish, for toilet paper, etcetera—
that has more praxis than all of killjoy Aquinas
or your hypocritical *isms* and movements that are wind from
the bottom! I therefore bequeath my washboard cranium to
the grinding incinerator of posterity.

Entelechy on the Libidinal Fringe

Ogot, you invertebrate charlatan!

Virtuoso of gibes, sexy bastard:
Your paradigm is the hermit crab . . .

Your omphalos tacked up primly for sale

Amid gobbledygook, guzzle of wits
Attenuated by Capital; arctic opulence
Proves plastic, protoplasmic
In an equipoise of hazards—

Peripeteia in flux, e.g.:
"Wyrda" used up to "weird"—

Ichor and/or ambrosia?

Ogot, don't monopolize the booze!

Three for the Road

The Black Masseur

Vainglory on terra firma—
Mr. Leeuwenhoek
Tabooed it.

Still the Devil quotes Scriptures—
The last shall be first, the first last:
Agendite of inwit.

Vanity? Don't sell out, capitalist dog!
The black masseur danced
Nude among giant ferns.

Anaximander, That Gay Fellow, Claims
All Men Descended from the Fish

Eels for breakfast?
Stranded on the shoals
Your vision circumscribes

Moby Dick for lunch—
So great a temptation. . . .
But sit pretty: don't despair.

"Unto us the bitter and gay"
Who witnessed loaves broken,
Serve piranha for supper.

Arse Phooooeeeey-tic-ah!

Jazzed up from Nowhere, your afflatus
Tunes in a flatulence
Syncopated with paroxysms of—

Or is the style gutsy, visceral?

The End of the Affair

On the ceiling of the dim pavilion
Where fire burns most deeply, you behold those inscrutable shapes
As if in a dream:
                          an iceberg on the great Salt Lake desert,
A hedgehog burrowing into its lunar hole. . . .

Palestrina's love, you hold yourself inviolable—
You would loose the prodigal stride of words
And stake the painstaking vision—

Diamond-edged splinter!
                        You would blind my will
To the stake on which your coquette heart kindles flesh
To violence, leaving only sunbleached fossils;

You've kept yourself cool, distinct, pure—
Preserved for Tammuz the centaur?
Or, the sun behind your shoulders burning,
Served before death around the mulberry bush?

E. SAN JUAN, JR. has published several collections of poetry in English and in Tagalog, including *God Kissing Carrion* (1964), *The Exorcism and Other Poems* (1967), *Kung Ikaw Ay Inaapi Bakit Hindi Ka Magbalikwas?* (1984), and *The Ashes of Pedro Abad Santos and Other Poems* (1985). He is also one of the Philippines' most esteemed critics and literary theorists publishing in the U.S. and abroad.

RICARDO M. DE UNGRIA

Culture Nervous

The mauve and printed silk go well
with your loneliness, lady.
African violets, are they?
I wouldn't think of plants
to honor an emotion,
or of clothes, or table settings.

We don't even have to play
at being formally into
ennui or anguish, as it were.
Imperatives gloss over
our last efficiencies, the
Bach Violin Concertos

Make sure we know. Or Sting?
Or Nine Inch Nails? Gnash not
the teeth of conscience hard—
there's middle age and mid-career yet
to focus us criminally
past our poverties and into our prime.

Let's see. When blackouts come
what hits you first—the fall of moral
categories or the contemplation of stars?
Do we begin something here
or wait by the window for sirens
to check out the gunshots next block?

If we love our wounds so much
and show these animals as a point

of honor, I'll stare all night
at the Warhol Monroe repro
while you work into lahar
your Lacan and Foucault.

Commerce and the Man

Today's Market-in-the-Loop finds the poet
sitting by the only table between the stalls.
White hair, crossed legs, cigarette in shaky hands
and a pacific professional half-smile
(unpoetlike, a gift from cheery depths)
indicate a daily serious business at hand.
He suns himself in the midmorning
give-and-take of shopper and seller,
the paper bags flapping open, money
changing hands, the smell of barbecue
fighting off the piscene fumes from the fish shop.
Some come prepared with lists, while others pick
on the spot, helped by their wives' mnemonics.
They might know him by hearsay or by sight,
but they try to politely ignore him.
They can't know possibly what to say to him,
or how approach him best without dissolving
the spell he seems lost in. And besides,
what has poetry to do with produce?
Their hands move past the bruised tomatoes
and into the okras and peppers and beans,
or else lift bananas to check on ripeness
and spots.

Yet they eye him from where they stand,
struck by his solitude's unstirring gaze,
to see if he has caught on to their lives
and arrived at a good-old rule-of-heart or two.
They feel absorbed in some ungospel truth,
some form of shapelessness they're living out
this very moment in someone else's eyes.
They feel contingent and cared for, eventful
and serviceable, themselves and not themselves.
Even the most philosophical and most revised
of them will say, This must be how it is—to be
just a word taking place among the human elements,
trying to mean even when no one is looking.
What life could I be leading in the poem
he is now making? What exception or rule
do I begin to share with that woman with zucchinis,
or this french bread, or those jars of mustard,
or the price tags stapled on the wooden beams?
When he gets up to go, what of me does he bring?
Will he write his poem? Can I recognize myself
when I read it? Can I say at least
I was there? Is there life after the poem?
Should it matter to me, or to anyone here?

When he pays and gets his change and takes his bag,
he looks again and sees the poet gone.
It'll be the death of me, he thinks, when I find
my thoughts expressed but clearer in his thoughts,
and my very words said in his own words
but more precise and musical than I
myself could ever manage. Then can I say
we've finally met without formal
introductions? or that we gave and we took
without real advantages? How can I
live my life placidly again? Already

I feel like a real living poet
but without the poet's way with words. But
thank God it's all over now. The world's at large
again and this just another morning.

Carillonneur

I took the thought
of going back to New York
for a walk at dawn
before the fruit vendors
set up their stalls
and while the she-wolf next door
is still making love
loudly for the good of us all.
Wind-whipped trash bags
winging down empty streets
still remain the sure signs
of the city's nursery of speed.

Someone must be keeping count
of what is yet to come.
So strong is the feeling
some long-overdue debt
is being paid me
in installments.
When I look at my photos and postcards
I know I have been somewhere,
and everything is still taking place
long enough for me
to move from here to there.

Making a home for absences
restores to the self the true
magnificence and pain of presence.
It gives me confidence
and drives me out to seek
inclemencies of love.

As long as I can keep from talking
to myself too long,
as long as passion kills
mutely and obscurely
I can live here.
But this can be anywhere,
the tambourines higher in pitch,
the bed harder.
And I find myself again
out of the A-train
in the middle of nowhere,
ready to begin again
with slick black hair.

Sui Veneris/The Poet of No Return

It is incessantly.
More than weekends at the beach, birthsigns, books
And the mind of candescent fingers
Seeking to soothe softnesses
Before the visions bubble to the head and openly weep.
That in the quick of this dark and the sprawl
Of her dance, she, now least attentive of all,
Falls into flesh. She with impatient certainties

196

And the lightness of heart washed in hues
As though passed through rose windows.
Whether, in the mystic gestures she alone has bones for,
She observes or is swayed by this priesthood of eyes
Is horizon and sky, postponing pinnacles
Of concussions and desire like the pout of lips
Pausing from saxophone reeds for breath.
It is mutinous—all completeness siphoned to her side!
The whole weight of her yet unfinished nakedness
Sampled like sunset of chronicles of a striptease
In the mind without cymbals or drums, only melodies.

Sheer with sibilants is this night's focus, convoked.
A thigh here Platonic, for a while there sonic crystals
Of a waist touched off a deflection of wrists.
And the knees would not stay. A nipple brief with censure
And a sketch of hair swear her musing welcome—
To lap the bathroom bulb's stammering light?
Her mind, like our coming to it in due time,
Without losing a beat gives descriptions a head
Traceable from fixed points o'ed in her mouth.
Very carefully. Her baby-sweet tongue rounds a bend,
Her outlines inherent in contraposto
Lower adagios to a norm. The climbing heat
Left to its foils, the trysts inlaid with rubies.

This must be how to sit unravelled like a crown
On the unconscious, or to feel space
Cross its own interstices without decay.
Do arcs of her muscles ever approach a list of errands
That will send any man out all day to collect,
Every day? And if called to the microphone,
What languages will they unclog from the landscape—
Such that memories, wild-eyed, will take their eyes off
Their chessboards for the first time?

Mute swoop of underbreasts! Under any light
Her coherence exhausts all sexual lore.
She hums now to herself as under the shower earlier,
And the silence after indents the domes
Of poetry and philosophy, scattering the birds.

Rut of jeans, undies and roaches on the floor.
What is air in this room, any room,
That is not her notion and neglect?
Absolute among the weeds is the sense of balance
Emerging from the undertow of walls.
Her lace of video screen rays is soaked with sweat,
She floats into view dripping with roused silhouettes.
Altering her nearness she purses her weakened circles
Towards the tested course.
Cleaves, to disencumber communion of its rails.
Like poles of the earth, perspectives tilt
Their frames and clear the ground on both ends
To accept the oscillation.

Breasts and raised arms the handcarved lines,
Topmost consonance of welcome and abeyance.
Ultimately her shadings and fermentations
Outpluralled the red cassette recorder
And plugged to its source integral music,
Inmost peg of transformations.
That way entered her thrusts counter, embossed
On pillows, pivoting on heels reachable,
The toes curled. Or else her thighs
In slow successive motions and designs intuited
From butterfly knives snapped and fanned open
Peel the pursuing definition to its pole
And the depth no longer withheld, to its moisture.
Would that these spirals, tumbling cones and rules
Of thumb send a revolution beyond its slogans!

198

All in the elbows and kneecaps rubbing the axis
Where uncertainties, hemmed in, ring most true,
Parallel with mutual codes, slender for the return,
Anaphora, cataphora, sweet Ipsithilla.

But now her hips sideways, tall as walls of Troy, signal
Shifts in directions, flow of heat, destinies.
Like mist crouching as if without strength
Is the moving without gaps against the tug of milk,
All of breath sluiced, spilling with every heave.
In the crushing openness is a mind for structures
Built only of nerves and concentration,
Sands and transparencies sifted in a blink of ultramarine
To keep the picture running full length.

That slidden away from measures and forms
And hollowed out by incandescent evanescings
In the widths of centuries one cannot even remember
Her name or its declensions, or the wires of inferences
Already everywhere, too late to sort out
Under the pores of a will several moons ahead
And still inescapable, freeing what it absorbs,
That all the fumes of pain and purity uncoil their hearts
Outside this moment's grain and aureole.
                              For the life! it spills.
For the web of it that will not snap but only sways.
So for the sway of it, and the shudder, at the edge,
The spilled threads and the spin of life!

The sheer momentum of it all, facing the sun,
Collects the surrendered skin.
Filaments that never crossed the eyelids'
Undersides leap about unsorted,
Lifted by their enormous sleeves.
Only the clenched teeth, or the bitten lips

Connect the heart to its pulsing, the shaken
Spaces to their breaths, harmonics of oranges.

Groans and grunts the monads that escape the blackness.
What is it that remains without meaning to,
Its botanies not of the marl
Yet intimate with it, that a singer one day
Will step into its star and name
The vanished vines of light
Love? Backseat Passion? Genesis?
Beer-joint spunk? Ghost of Death?
Cup of Tea?
                            Incessantly.
It is God's cut glass and plate of meat,
And we know it good!
A finger to the heavens, a turd on the ground,
And we know it good!
In the gurgle of deep, extremest unctions
And the closures of grace it is good.
In the slight salinities of her
Still straddling the taste buds,
In the teethmarks stellified beyond ache,
The vise and the grinding without bones,
The flesh of depths torn open each time
Stern with a different power,
Bottomless with a different soul. It is good!

In the surfaceless moment where all being there subsides,
Blankets, warned of fatal substances, find us
Terminal nudes, finished prayers under dead stars,
Lying on our backs, slowly admitting back to flesh
Lost proportions and gravities
Behind cigarette smoke and a Bosphorus of thoughts,
The otherness emptied into its opposite,
Reflections adjusting themselves inside the eyes.

Tonight the edge of the city leaves a trail
Crossed many times over: through mineral mazes
Of neons, quibblings among the lawless and the drunk,
Preamps and pickups rooting for strife
In any close-packed bar and cocktail lounge.
Already it cuts across the whole emotion
Like a looking back, or a way to feel exempt
From principles of chemistry, weather, ownership.
Quicker than permanence drying like ink,
Words are first to leave for coffee and meanings.
Sidelong glances exchanged, like scriptures
Of God's silence and dreams, go back beyond
First introductions, initial subtleties, come-ons.
Static on the radio now, moonlight on the roofs,
Plash and tinkle in the courses of planets.
Yet between our hands retrieved from the other
The groinwarmth hammers a ciborium of space
Where the sky retains a blue above this night
And the slippery shine of celestial rims
Domes her as she unsnarls and rises,
Patting her hair, to open a window,
Draw air to breathe, implicate in her warmth
Accretions of feelings and affections snug
With the motes on the screen and grillwork.
The tug of tenderness dug up, the whole of it
And point of view, lifts her with the stealth
Of reverie beyond any name she will answer to,
Beyond all senses of the ordinary
That now wins her back.
In the course of which she might sing
And divine the lines of vision that lead outside
The frame, tracking her down
To her intimate details and vanishing points.
As now uncontained she sings, fuck-fresh and profane,
And leaves me the fragrance and the stain.

RICARDO M. DE UNGRIA received an MFA in Creative Writing from Washington University in St. Louis and is Chair of the Department of Arts and Communication at the University of the Philippines, Manila. He has written three collections of poetry, *Decimal Places* (1991), *Voideville: Selected Poems 1974-79* (1991), and *R+A+D+I+O* (1986). Among his many awards is a Manila Critics' Circle National Book Award in 1992.

MANUEL A. VIRAY

The Two Strangers

. . . in whom I am well pleased.

Peregrinus A:

The center,
the center of order
is lodged   in this
here   pair:

one yearning: the other, yielding;
they are also separate numbers, if, at
times, apart, together, jostling, joshing,
jumping, jiving, jamming,

silent, articulating, dancing, distressing fi-

gures
bodies,
But really,
just two quotients, numbers,
yang and yin.
They are wondrous because
of the secrets, miracles
they hide, expose.

Both, along with the dreamers and deluded,
move in whirling, interloping, anxious worlds,
inner
&
outer.

There are also the myths, the legendary worlds,
planet and asteroid where you and I
and the sky

h
a
n
g

f
r
o
m
.

How can the world be cold, chilly? Impel wonder,
defacements, deformity? It is less
warm and burning because of
aborted imperatives by
the neglectful,
the neglected,
the resentful, profligate, inside and
outside the iron gate.

The nobility, the distinctions go on, go on,
the luster, the habits, the apparentness, temporal, halt,
hesitant and sad, in pathetic intervals.

There's   geographical
the deceptive   and human,
season   brittle,

                    temporal:
          fertile,
                              disjunctive,
                                   generative.

There's   and of logic,
the legend   fissured,
of reason: fragile.

There's the unknown, eternal. The contextual.
        There's the sense of the *res ipsa,*
            the human; the enigma.

    The vibrations continue: a priori, in beginnings,
mating, adumbrations, anxieties and abracadabras, con-
flicts, confusion, wreaths and candelabrums - -
            through it all
        His breath, yours, mine,
            his, hers, theirs, ours,
                insistent, insistent,
                    if
                endangered.

    The vibration courses through from the center,
        goes on in seemingly ordered confusion.

            Where does it start, anyway?
                Where's its focus?
        The beautiful, the banal, the bitter? The
            pessimist, the ugly, the sinister?

Does it start from the heart, which may well be
            the terrain of dreams, doubt, and questioning:
            the unknown? Does it go past the ribs, up
            and around the shoulders, jump at random
            to other unexpected places, into the flesh?
            Into the flesh, into the veins and arteries?
            Going to and from the limbs, arms, fingers?
            Into the angered fist? The equilibrium, the
            heavenliness and appetites of the senses.

205

The dormant or apathetic will. Yet heaven
and earth and humans are never still. Can
the vibration touch, shake the far-seeing,
the microscopic eyes? The vision, amid the
fragrance, scent, stink of the human? The
sounds and resonances of hoarding and excited
avidities, anxieties? The bitten tongue, the
silent lips, the calm and ire of thought and
articulation?

Peregrinus B:

This is the dreamer. The noble, naive, godly,
    simple, dirty, crazy, elusive creature.
    Harried, subject to the code of conscious-
    ness and chimera, the magic of wonder and
    meanderings
            -

            -

                            _____

                                _____

                                    ____

                                        __

                                    ____

                            _____

                _____

Lost is he in his dreams, intent,
    resiliences, unexpected
    concessions, dementia,
    and disjunctives . . .
    lost is he . . .

Is he looking at the reflection of His
    gorgeousness? The light changes
    after it strikes the mirror,

the glass, the frangible flesh;
the reflection of lustrous germi-
nation and lost genealogies. And
what is the difference between
the curse and blessing?

And who should he ask, request to assist
him? The Holy Spirit? Should
the Holy Spirit plead, intervene for
him? The continuance of resolution,
remembrance, resonances?

The trees like the body bend with the wind.
Not the cross. Not the human.

> *. . . in whom I am well pleased.*

O, he thinks he knows the secret labyrinths
of the human body: the puzzle and conundrum
of the gene and cell; "the blessedness and
malediction of fire," deception and curse
of wind and water; grace of sky and cons-
tellations; essence of breath and atmos-
phere. He assumes limitless or outer
space on his side. He does not know that
the flames burst in the heat of the avid
embrace, the selfish probe into the ima-
gined universe of his consciousness and
sensuousness.

He thinks he knows the means and measures
dream and distress demand. He thinks
he knows the technology life and death
require.

This is my beloved son, in whom I am well pleased.

He thinks he knows himself, the godliness
                and the Holy Spirit. He does not know
                I am ahead. I am ahead.
                He's more dead than alive. During the
                day or night, "graveyard shift."
                Or on duty from twelve noon to twelve
                midnight. Seven to seven. Five to five.

Patio

The light silently shifts even as three kittens leap,
skitter through the patio, accenting the afternoon's
orange glow; the wind veers, skips from variants of
thought, queries, elusive clue.

    The air conditioner resumes its hum.
    I keep adjusting its center to consequence its function.

    On the windowsill a potted plant with curving stems
with struggling leaves disturbs a puzzling fragment in
the fringe of the mind—ecdysiast of search and wonder-
ment.

    Out in the patio straggling in the unusual summery
heat of September, the searching eye, uneasy, questing,
pauses, jumps over the weathered fence, framing lustrous
hibiscus and marigold, past the brooding leafy oak, goes
towards, the tarnished two-story apartment building, three
windows opened, late laundry hanging on a line. It gra-

vitates towards a missing focus, draws back, oscillates
in the air, querying mind, the fence, the tiny garden
plot. Where then does wandering begin wondering end?

   Always are there sudden thought, hiding insight, a
baffling line, cluster of carousels and disturbances;
continuous irritation, and anger at impulsions and inner
implosions, dividing object, eye, heart and complaints.
Judgment or reaction is never a concentrate, accrual of
of scenes: time enchanting, if cruel, is irrepres-
sible; quiet, then volatile; we forget refrains,
recurrences, repetitions, resentments.

               *   *   *

               If

during the conception of, or by hibiscus
and marigold, there form seductive, exqui-
site shapes and colors, will these later
than sooner lure, tempt the philosopher,
unsuspecting lovers with compounds or
complex, complicities of ecstasies, mean-
derings, and apothegms?

         Can you or I
still jump out of our origins, shelters,
or skins, tithed radiance, wish and impa-
tience; welter of cruelty, regret, desire,
               the folly of anger?

         There are
attractive, mesmerizing shifts,
splendor and disturbance
in the unusual September weather.
               They throw

riddles to the philosopher,
who looks beyond a lover, lovers,
all impulsions, grafting air and
            atmosphere,
            who looks beyond
barbaric theories, frazzled fathers,
sons and daughters, the sane, the saint
and sinners who, in sudden apprehension,
perception of our carelessness,
agenda and conclusions,
disdained, disregarded,
derided, discarded, deflected
insistence of grace and equilibrium,
            still live out,
                  live out
your and my abstractions;
temporal weather, inner and outer,
            outer and inner,
fever, indifference, pollutions,
pallidities, nuclear and antinuclear
energies, fission,
      autumn,
            summer,
                  spring,
                        and winter.

A Saturday Morning

From some void,
                    nothingness
the first hour of day, actually
the first pinkish scarlet circle
of light this sudden wintry morning
        reverses
impatience and blankness, then turns
to anger close to irony
        but
the perception,
the paradox,
the shift and motion
of persons, kith, kin or
relatives, friends, strangers
linger,
            malinger
with purposes heaved, fragmented;
        secret dreams thrown, segmented

            .   .   .

You've to attend to first things
        first, but isn't
        the last the first?
            both
starting from these myths:
breath, motion, shifts, motionlessness,
extravaganzas, extortionists, essences,
        existentialists,
                        wreaths?

And isn't the Garden a fable,
        legend, an exploding secrecy,
        expediency, trembling tradition,
        provocation, doubt, dissimulation?
                Alarum.
                Minatory vibrations.
        Hidden acts and/or deceptions of
        sons, daughters, sisters, inter-
                lopers.
                Centrum.
        Force unseen, adherence of dying
        flesh to disturbed bones shake
                perceptions, apothegms,
                and paradigms.

        .   .   .   .

Have closed territories behind me;
        not Charles Simic's doubt
        about the existence of
        Point A, he had just left
        and Point B, which he thought,
        he would see by and by: but these
        do not exist. He refutes this
        theory, damnation, distress.
        Insists on the presence of dreams.
But in the peaceful or disturbed atmosphere.
        solar and lunar, to mortality's fatal
        dynamics, transient magic there occur
        silent subtle shifts, secret trans-
        formations, metamorphoses. Of flesh
        to lust or deadliness; love to cruel
        dubieties; unforeseen distress;
        appearance of desire and deformations,
        gasps, fading breaths, the inexplicable
        chloroform of vanishing forms.

From here, from an anonymous address on w 37th Street
   the sudden
         d
        a
       z
       z
        l
         e
          m
           e
            n
             t
  of winter
       c
       a
      s
       t
      s

a heavenly glow past the languid
  fence on the bare brooding oak tree, a
  neighbor's smudged rotting window.
I now stand on the portico, uneasy with absence
  of immediate readings of shifting
  phenomena, worlds dreamt of but never
  bared, disclosed, or made.
Suddenly on the other side of the street there
  appear three black children and a white
  blond-haired kid with their mother?
  going for early morning milk, an 85-cent
  loaf of bread, butter from the Seven/Eleven
  in our neighborhood.
The senses pulse, the mind roils; Utrillo's
  linear and/or inner perspective returns
  to me, retraces another sudden morning

radiance: wintry sun shining on two black
babies in green winter wraps and caps in
two green carriages, pushed by two black
mothers also in capes and caps of verdant
green.

The morning appears suspended:
there's a magnificent whiff of caressing
wind, morning adoration this early
Saturday morning.

MANUEL A. VIRAY was born in 1917 in Lingayen, Pangasinan. He received a
PhD from the University of the Philippines in 1936, taught at several universi-
ties, but eventually opted for a career in the Philippine Foreign Service, attain-
ing the post of Ambassador to Cambodia 1973-1975. He is one of the country's
most important poet-critics to come out of the post-World War II generation.
He was the first literary critic of the forties and fifties to document, contextu-
alize, and clarify the literature of his contemporaries in anthologies such as
Heart of the Island: An Anthology of Philippine Poetry in English (1947) and the
Philippine Poetry Annual 1947-1949 (1950). His collections of poetry include
After This Exile (1963), *Where Blood with Light Collides* (1975), and *Morning
Song* (1990). He lives in Virginia Beach, Virginia.

ALFRED YUSON

Andy Warhol Speaks to His Two Filipino Maids

Art, my dears, is not cleaning up
after the act. Neither is it washing off
grime with the soap of tact. In fact
and in truth, my dears, art is dead,

center, between meals, amid spices
and spoilage. Fills up the whitebread
sweep of life's obedient slices.

Art is the letters you send home
about the man you serve. Or the salad
you bring in to my parlor of elites.
While Manhattan stares down at the soup

of our affinities. And we hear talk of coup
in your islands. There they copy love
the way I do, as how I arrive over and over

again at art. Perhaps too it is the time
marked by the sand in your shoes, spilling
softly like rumor. After your hearts I lust.
In our God you trust. And it's your day off.

Dead Center

Spent a night in Pratt, Kansas.
On a queen-sized bed in a quiet motel.
Giant TV glared down at a fearsome cant from the ceiling.

Tired from the drive, hungry in the cold,
I went up Main Street (others there seemed
in dark peripheries) and stopped by the neons
of a pizza parlor. Took back the crusty prize
along with a postcard that said this town
was the geographic center of Mainland USA.

Burped roadmaps of anchovies and mushrooms,
washed the garlic down with Pabst Blue Ribbon.
Lay back until the mesmeric box in the overhang
lulled me to a dead center sleep and a dead
center dream on the queen-sized bed
in a quiet motel on Main Street, dead center USA.

Love before Dinner

She said she'd do
Peking Duck
for dinner.
When I saw her
train the hair dryer
on the hookbound fowl
I conceded—such was
the crisp skin of love

216

I felt for her.
The scene was one
of ageless ardor.
As when we blow
whiffs of fancy
towards affection
in some delicate hour
of sacrament—the sauce
imagined over and over.

World Poetry Circuit

1. The Poets Arrive and Shake Hands

2. The Poets Receive Their Breakfast Coupons

3. The Poets Listen to Speeches

4. The Poets Take Their Own Turns Onstage

5. The Poets Attend A Garden Reception

6. The Poets Line Up for The Prince

7. The Poets Are Taken to A Beach Resort

8. The Poets Are Caught Up in Traffic

9. The Poets Pose for A Group Shot

10. The Poets Land in the Papers

ALFRED YUSON has received several Palanca Memorial Awards. He has distinguished book publications in many genres, including *Great Philippine Energy Cafe* (novel, 1987), *The Music Child & Other Stories* (short fiction, 1991), *Confessions of a Q.C. Househusband* (essays, 1991), *Sea Serpent* (poems, 1993). His poems have been published in U.S. journals such as *The Iowa Review*, *Frank*, and *Manoa*. He lives in Quezon City, Metro Manila.

R. ZAMORA-LINMARK

Day I: Portrait of the Artist, Small-kid Time

I.
When I was in fifth grade,
Miss K. made us write a poem
for the State Annual Poetry
Contest, Division III.

. . . if you're chosen, $100.00 . . .

Our eyes went
bonkers. Our faces wore
a hundred-dollar smile.
Even "Twinkles" Batongbacal's packed-on
make-up and "Honeygirl" Perez's scotch-
taped eyelids were peeled off
by the crisp Ben Franklin.

. . . read your poem out loud . . . top three . . .

We all gave the evil-
eye to each other, thinking,
Eh, wot? You tink you one poet?
No ways, Joses. I get da last word.
We walked around with an I-spit-
on-your-poem-attitude, except
to Jennifer Stewart cuz she was the only one
who could speak, read, write
English right.

II.
I told Miss K. I did not
know what to write
              so
she popped a quarter out.
"Here, catch the 52 Circle Island. Write
    'bout the people on the bus,
        study their faces,
          and write.
              If
            you're
          still stuck,
        ask for a transfer
    and keep riding the pen."

III.
For one week, we hid
our frustrations, our insecurities,
and spilled them out
in 6th period P.E. with sham-
battle, German dodge-
ball, flag football,
and every ball you could
possibly think of.

IV.
When time came,
everyone went up:

Jr. Santiago, the only Filipino who had enough courage to admit
        he ate black dogs, wrote 'bout his first time at a cock-
        fight in Waipahu.

Edward Caraang, III wrote 'bout coming to America and
        shopping at Gem's.

Lisa Ann "Honeygirl" Perez wrote 'bout her third time with her
        babe Darren.

Frank Concepcion wrote 'bout being an altar boy in the
        Philippines and the fun he had with the priests who
        played with him and let him sleep over.

Cary Kaneshiro wrote 'bout winning the Chinese jacks
        competition.

Randall Keola Lim wrote 'bout his first time with "Honeygirl"
        Perez inside the big cannon in front of Fort DeRussy.

Swee Ming "Suzanne" Low wrote 'bout Dim Sum.

Darren Sipili wrote 'bout beefing Randall after school.

Kalani "Babes" Alu, my best friend, wrote 'bout surfing
        at the North Shore with the tsunami waves breaking the
        bones.

Pedro "Boo" Arucan wrote 'bout his rose-tattooed chest.

Domingo Bocalbos wrote 'bout the uninvited bees who wrecked
        his birthday picnic, grinding all the lumpias, pansit,
        and pig's blood.

Jennifer Stewart wrote 'bout the military importance in Hawaii.

Mary Ann Fujimoto wrote 'bout spending x-mas at Hale Kipa
        cuz her mother lost it after her "other half" croaked from
        crystal meth.

Tyrone "Foots" White wrote 'bout being Popolo in Kalihi.

Joey "Boogaloo" Silva wrote 'bout winning the 1st Annual
     Break-dancing Competition held at the State Capitol.

Mataele Mataele wrote 'bout this road in the deep end of the
     valley diverging and he could not figure out which one to
     take, so he took the path that was less familiar, that had
     less footprints, and he ended up in Kahuku.

Purificacion "Twinkles" Batongbacal wrote 'bout her sixth time.

     Except me.

v.
I wrote 'bout

Hungry bees eating space, black dogs losing it first time.

America raiding scotch-taped Kalihi while Pedros drowned
     in Franco's German-spit second time.

Dim in the Philippines, P.I. Joes missing in Fort Derussy's
     dead-end pockets third time.

Immigrants coming to Kalihi twinkling with their American
     crystal meth dream fourth time.

Smiles that can break evil bones after school, culture
     break-dancing beef in front of Gem's fifth time.

Uninvited priests with their rose tattooes, grinding fighting
     cocks and preaching last words on a hundred dollar
     altar sixth time.

(And I wrote 'bout pig cap pen bleeding a hundred dollar poem.)

election day

it's 7 a.m. mother, the walking
alarm clock, goes off, hollering
and bitching about the dent
on her mustang lx and threatening
to destroy my license and me.

get a grip, ma.

it's 7 a.m. and the last thing
i need right now is her
screaming lungs
complaining how life is never fair,
how she does not deserve
this kind of treatment, especially
from her son—how she does not
give a flying fuck who wins
the presidential election today
because she thinks everyone
is screwed.

i guess she's not voting.

why is she doing
this to me? three shots
of jack daniels last night.
i'm hung over and she's still
bitching about her car.
i've got so many things to do.
i shouldn't have gone out
last night, but i did
because i really wanted to,
even if i have a paper

to write, and *sons*
and lovers to read. i should
have stayed home but i went
out anyway because today
is election day.

i'm voting none of the above.

i hate voting, i hate
papers, i never cared about
poetry, and i wish d.h. wrote
novels with illustrations.
but most of all, i wish someone
would shut her up. she is still
screeching like a souped-
up camaro burning rubber.

i cannot believe i'm listening
to her, a.k.a. the quint-
essential hag of waipahu
lecturing me on how to grow up.

enough.

how do you shut
her up? why do i keep
calling her "mother?"
she never baked
cookies. she bought them
next door at the family
store run by koreans, and threw
them on the table, pointing
in her loud contralto voice,
HERE'S YOUR GODDAMN CHIPS
AHOY. she screamed

when i ate everything, left
her the crumbs, and exploded—
burning me with WHERE'S MY DAMN
CHIPS AHOY?

it's almost 7:30 a.m.
and the moon's still
up but slowly fading
away. my roommate's still
sleeping, snoring musically.
he starts softly and crescendos
until he can't reach the next
octave or i shut him up.

i wish mother would give

up soon and say BYE but i
know she's not going
to let me off easy. i have
to tell her i am wrong.
she'll laugh and tell me,
I TOLD YOU SO.

mother enjoys punishing.
when i was young, she'd beat
me up and tell me afterwards,
soft and gentle,
HONEY, I ONLY DID IT
BECAUSE I LOVE YOU.
i'd believe her, try
to be good but she'd go off
her rocker and keep hitting
me until neighbors finally called
the child protection agency.
when that happened, mother

stampeded out of the house
and into the street, yelling,
WHO THE FUCK REPORTED ME?
we ended up in court, scared,
and i had to tell them
i loved her.

jesus, the hangover
is getting worse, my head
spinning, pulling me wherever
gravity is. if i don't get some
rest right now, i'll be a walking
cabbage the whole day.

but why should i
give in to her? now
she's asking me stupid
questions and answering
them herself. DO YOU KNOW
WHY YOU'RE IN SUCH GOOD SHAPE?
I'LL TELL YOU WHY.
IT'S BECAUSE I RAISED YOU,
DAMNIT! AND NOW YOU
TREAT ME LIKE SHIT.

i'm fleshed out.
should just apologize
about the dent on her
car. tell her it was not
my fault. she's not
going to listen to me.
oh, no. not now. she's
on the ball, rambling, giving
me the diarrhea of the mouth.

she stops only to see
if i'm still on and i say,
YES, MOTHER and she goes
on, talking to herself.

this is too much.
the pressure in my head
is throbbing, veins
pop out, eyeballs pop out.
i tell her, I'M SORRY.
AND I LOVE YOU.

stop.

i hate this part
because she starts in on how
she's so proud of me,
how she's so lucky
to have a gifted child, how
she's so proud of being a mother,
even though the p.t.a. voted her
the worst mother for three years
consecutively and she was forced
to join alcoholics anonymous.
she says they're history and don't matter
now because she's cured. i tell her
again how sorry i am, how much
i love her, and finally,
she hangs
up.

R. ZAMORA-LINMARK's first novel, *Rolling the R's*, was published by Kaya Productions in 1995. His prose and poetry have been included in the anthologies *Charlie Chan Is Dead* and *Ladlad: Anthology of Philippine Gay Writings*. He lives in Honolulu, Hawaii.

Manila Paper

No wonder I'm a poet.
I used to sit in my high chair and recite
at the dinner table every night.
I was the opening act
for the headliner, my dad.
He ruled the clan
like Olivier in Camelot.
I banged my spoon
while he told war stories.
That was his forté,
how he saved a mother and child from the Japanese
by hiding them under a mattress.
He was a doctor doing his job.
His job was saving lives.

Mom was the expert
at telling ghost stories.
She could curl your hair
with hoary tales of her childhood in Leyte—
the night a hairy monster
breathed under her bed.

My schtick went like this:

"There was a little girl
who had a little curl
right in the middle of her forehead.
When she was good,
she was very very good
but when she was bad,
she was horrid."

That was me.
Still is
to this day.

No matter what I do,
I can't get over me.
I'm cursed and destined
to talk to myself
for the rest of my life,
and the next one
and the next one.

There I'll be
up on that eternal kindergarten stage
in my white cotton pinafore,
white crenolins,
white socks,
white shoes.

There I'll be
up on that stage,
two front teeth missing
but going on anyway,
floating in a black hole,
dazed by the lights,
lisping my s's,
searching the crowd
for Mom and Dad,
some familiar face,
stealing the show,
the show that must go on.

After all,
what's a few teeth
among poets?

once upon a seesaw with charlie chan

i think i was three
beneath the guava tree
next to the doghouse in the front yard
with the crisscross bamboo fence
the seesaw was pastel
pink green and yellow
and i a nut brown child with brown hair
i had the up-and-down-of-it down pat
as i straddled the wooded plank with chubby knees
facing a boy nicknamed charlie chan
it was a slow afternoon
wives winning at majong
maids eavesdropping
i may have been daydreaming
of the other playground
the one with the swings and silver seesaws
the one that survived the tornado
or maybe my mind lingered
on the fingering of a piano
a blue dragonfly whizzing nearby
i soared above it all
above the red hibiscus flowers
and the sweet banana tree
above the bougainvillea and the gardenia
charlie had beads for eyes
that was how he got his name
he was smaller than i
and i was the girl
i don't know what got into him
as evenly weighted we swung side by side
he jumped on his seat like satan
up smack between my legs

a wooden whack drew blood
i searched for the trickled source
no wound or cut
no sign of origin
i ran to mother
she swabbed me with alchohol and muttered
no explanation
the bleeding stopped
there was no pain
and i never seesawed with charlie chan again

My Worst Fear

is that one day they'll win
one day those people
who always get in my way
will all get together in one room
and have a good time
for the first time
in their lives
all my enemies
those smiling men and women
in unimaginative attire
will win the Lotto
and spend it
on promotional materials
besmirching my good name
they'll have the last word
'cause i won't be there
to defend myself
or ignore them

listen to their noise
their petty envies
all my friends will be out of town
or worse
they won't speak up
they'll sit on their asses
and order another drink
or go shopping
or something

my worst fear
is that one day they'll win
i'll be a 400-pound couch potato
in a room with no window
only cable tv and cheap ice cream
i'll be watching the reruns of old movies
'cause by this time
i'd have seen every movie ever made
even the kung fu flicks
i'll be talking to my imaginary spouse in my sleep
and wake up as marlon brando
with no tarita or tahiti to come home to
i'd be alone
and i'd like it
better than sex

CYN. ZARCO's first collection of poetry, *cir'cum*nav'i*ga'tion* (1986) won an American Book Award from the Before Columbus Foundation. *Wild Style* (Simon & Schuster, 1986), her book of photographs on pop fashion, was published to critical acclaim. Her photographs have appeared in such magazines as *Interview* and *Us*. She works as a journalist and photographer and currently lives in Miami, Florida.

Acknowledgements

Gemino H. Abad. "The Light in One's Blood," "Toys," and "Jeepney" first published in *Solidarity*. Reprinted by permission of the author. "Holy Order" used by permission of the author.

Karina Africa-Bolasco. "Sauna 2" first published in *Forbidden Fruit: Women Write the Erotic/An Anthology* (Anvil, 1992). Reprinted by permission of the author.

Carlos A. Angeles. "Light Invested" first published in *Philippine Panorama*, February, 1993; "Words" first published in *Philippine Panorama*, December, 1993. Reprinted by permission of the author.

Mila D. Aguilar. "Pall Hanging over Manila" and "Poem from Sierra Madre" from *A Comrade Is as Precious as a Rice Seedling* (Kitchen Table: Women of Color Press). Copyright © 1984 by Mila D. Aguilar. Reprinted by permission of the author and of Kitchen Table: Women of Color Press, Box 40-4920, Brooklyn, NY 112400-4920.

Maria Luisa B. Aguilar-Cariño. "Familiar" and "Dinakdakan" first published in *Asian Pacific American Journal*, Spring/Summer, 1994. Reprinted by permission of the author. "For the Lover" and "Gabi" used by permission of the author.

Nerissa S. Balce. "Pizza and Pretense" first published in *Forbidden Fruit: Women Write the Erotic/An Anthology* (Anvil, 1992). Reprinted by permission of the author.

JoAnn Balingit. "Quiet Evening, Home Away" used by the permission of the author.

Merlinda Bobis. "Word Gifts for an Australian Critic" and "Driving to Katoomba" used by permission of the author.

Rofel G. Brion. "Lover Song" and "One Morning beside a Pond" first published in *Baka Sakali* (1989); "Good Friday" and "If Fortune Smiles" first published in *Luna Caledonia* (1992). Reprinted by permission of the author.

Maria Elena Caballero-Robb. "Memoranda for Rosario" and "Dear Rosario" used by permission of the author.

Luis Cabalquinto. "Depths of Fields" first published in *Heritage Quarterly*, March, 1992; "The Ordinance" first published in *Trafika*, Autumn, 1993, reprinted by permission of the author. "The Value Added in Smashing a German Roach on the Bathroom Door" used by permission of the author.

Regie Cabico. "An Afternoon in Pangasinan with No Electricity" first published in *Ikon*, #14/15, 1994; "Check One" first published in *Aloud: Voices from the Nuyorican Poets Cafe* (Heny Holt, 1994). Reprinted by permission of the author.

Eugene Gloria. "Touch" first appeared in *Philippine Free Press,* October 1993; "Aleng Maria" first appeared in *Philippine Graphic,* January, 1994; "Rizal's Ghost" first appeared in *Mid-American Review,* Vol. xiv, 1993. Reprinted by permission of the author. "Assimilation" used by permission of the author.

N.V.M. Gonzalez. "A Wanderer in the Night of the World," "The Deepest Well in Madras," "How the Heart Aches," and "I Made Myself a Path" used by permission of the author.

Vince Gotera. "Madarika" first published in *Dissident Song: A Contemporary Asian American Anthology* (a double issue of *Quarry West,* U.C. Santa Cruz) Volume 29/30, 1991 and also reprinted in *The Open Boat: Poems from Asian America,* edited by Garrett Hongo (Anchor/Doubleday, 1993); "Pacific Crossing" first published in *Liwanag,* Vol. ii (San Francisco, 1995). Reprinted by permission of the author. "Manong Chito Tells Manong Ben about His Dream over Breakfast at the Manilatown Cafe" and "First Mango" used by permission of the author.

Jessica Hagedorn. "Souvenirs," copyright © 1975 by Jessica Hagedorn; "Vulva Operetta" copyright © 1993 by Jessica Hagedorn, from *Danger and Beauty* by Jessica Hagedorn. Used by permission of Viking Penguin, a division of Penguin Books usa Inc.

Alejandrino G. Hufana. "The Insides of Alfred Hitchcock," "From the Raw," "Contemporary," and "Floating Epitaphs, Their Possible Explanations in Poro Point" used by permission of the author.

Dolores de Iruretagoyena de Humphrey. "No Immunity" and "Hope" first published in *Poems for the Heart and Voice* (Cuernavaca, Mexico, 1986). Copyright 1986 by Dolores de Iruretagoyena de Humphrey. Reprinted by permission of the author. "April in Houston" used by permission of the author.

Dominador I. Ilio. "Marikudo in Kalibo, 1979," "Children of the Atomic Age," "Prokosch in Tehran, 1978," and "The Site of My Grandfather's House" first published in *Collected Poems of Dominador I. Ilio* (Quezon City, Philippines, 1989). Copyright © 1989 by Dominador I. Ilio. Reprinted by permission of the author.

Jaime Jacinto. "Tongue Tied," "Heaven Is Just Another Country," "Absence," and "Visitation" used by permission of the author.

Fatima Lim-Wilson. "Alphabet Soup (Mimicry as a Second Language)" first appeared in *Crosscurrents;* "The Beginning of Things" and "Ringmaster's Wife" first appeared in *Prairie Schooner;* "Raising the Dead" first appeared in *Poetry.* Reprinted by permission of the author.

Michael Melo. "Unlearning English" first published in *ZYZZYVA,* Summer, 1993; "Red Lipstick on a Straw" first published in *Spillway,* Spring, 1995. Reprinted by permission of the author. "Scrambled Eggs and Garlic Pork" used by permission of the author.

Noel Mateo. "There Is No Word for Sex in Tagalog" and "Jeepneyfying" used by permission of the author.

Clovis L. Nazareno. "Bohol's Tarsier Population" and "The Cortes Swamp" used by permission of the author.

Yolanda Palis. "Waking Up" and "The Floor" used by permission of the author.

Patrick Pardo. "Untitled" first published in *420 Magazine,* Spring, 1992. Reprinted by permission of the author.

Bino A. Realuyo. "The Sojourners" and "La Querida" used by permission of the author.

Danton Remoto. "Rain" first published in *Skin Voices Faces* (Anvil, 1991). Copyright © 1991 by Danton Remoto. Reprinted by permission of the author. "Exile," "Black Silk Pajamas," and "Images of John (1967-92)" used by permission of the author.

Al Robles. "remembering the past" first published in *Amerasia Journal,* 1989. Reprinted by permission of the author. "Feasting with Etang a Hundred Times Around," "Cutting Back the Ifugao Past," and "The Manong with a Thousand Tribal Visions" used by permission of the author.

E. San Juan, Jr. "The Owl of Minerva Takes Flight in the Evening," "Entelechy on the Libidinal Fringe," "Three for the Road," and "The End of the Affair" used by permission of the author.

Ricardo M. De Ungria. "Commerce and the Man," "Carillonneur," and "Sui Veneris/The Poet of No Return" first published in *Decimal Places* (Anvil). Copyright © 1991 by Ricardo M. De Ungria. Reprinted by permission of the author. "Culture Nervous" used by permission of the author.

Manuel A. Viray. "The Two Strangers," "Patio," and "A Saturday Morning" used by permission of the author.

Alfred Yuson. "Andy Warhol Speaks to His Two Filipino Maids," "Dead Center," "Love before Dinner," and "World Poetry Circuit" first published in *Trading in Mermaids* (Anvil). Copyright © 1993 by Alfred Yuson. Reprinted by permission of the author.

R. Zamora-Linmark. "Day 1: Portrait of the Artist, Small-kid Time" first appeared in *Willow Springs;* "election day" first appeared in *Asian Pacific American Journal,* Summer, 1993. Reprinted by permission of the author.

cyn. zarco. "once upon a seesaw with charlie chan" first published in *cir'cum*nav'i*ga'tion* (Tooth of Time Books, 1986). Copyright © 1986 by cyn. zarco. Reprinted by permission of the author. "Manila Paper" and "My Worst Fear" used by permission of the author.

COLOPHON

The text of this book was set in Garamond type. Coffee House books are printed on acid-free paper and are smyth sewn for durability and reading comfort.